THE NATURE OF TRUE VIRTUE

THE NATURE
OF TRUE VIRTUE

by JONATHAN EDWARDS

With a Foreword by William K. Frankena

ANN ARBOR PAPERBACKS

THE UNIVERSITY OF MICHIGAN PRESS

First edition as an Ann Arbor Paperback 1960
Third printing 1966
Foreword © by The University of Michigan 1960

Published in the United States of America by
The University of Michigan Press and simultaneously
in Rexdale, Canada, by Ambassador Books Limited
Manufactured in the United States of America

FOREWORD

by William K. Frankena

JONATHAN EDWARDS (1703–58) was for a long time thought of rather as a preacher of revival and hell-fire than as a theologian, and rather as a Calvinistic theologian than as a philosopher of importance, and he was dismissed accordingly. Yet, as is now increasingly realized, he was perhaps the outstanding American theologian and certainly the ablest American philosopher to write before the great period of Peirce, James, Royce, Dewey, and Santayana. In no field is his power more manifest than in moral philosophy. Even here, however, he has been known mainly for his book on the freedom of the will, which has usually been shrugged off as a defense of the outdated doctrine of predestination, but is recently being recognized again as a remarkable piece of philosophy. But Edwards did also write a smaller systematic treatise on ethics proper, called *The Nature of True Virtue*. Although not widely read, it has been said to have few peers in the field of ethics; and, whether this is true or not, it is a philosophical work of great originality and penetration, which deserves to be ranked with anything written on the same subject by any of the more recent Americans just referred to. That is why it is here being made

v

available again, complete and in a separate binding for the first time.

The Nature of True Virtue was written in 1755, though some of the ideas in it were already put down in "Notes on the Mind" when Edwards was still a mere youth. It did not appear in his lifetime, presumably because he was not yet satisfied with it. In 1765 it was published posthumously together with another short dissertation, *Concerning the End for Which God Created the World,* to which it makes reference on one or two occasions.

Because of when and by whom it was written, our essay has theological passages and overtones which may put some readers off. Edwards was a Calvinist, perhaps the best philosopher Calvinism ever produced, and he wrote primarily to defend his theological position. Yet he was a philosopher, and a bold and independent one; he meant to propound an ethical theory which was consistent with Calvinism, but he meant to establish it on empirical and rational grounds, even if he does refer to Scripture once or twice. In doing so he produced a work which is interesting and important apart from any connection it may have with his theology, simply as a piece of moral philosophy. This is true even if there are points in it where he takes a position which is required by Calvinism without giving any very good arguments for it; even at these points what he says is penetrating and stimulating in its own right and may possibly be correct. At least it is not always obvious that the alternative position is on any better footing philosophically.

However, in this day of Barths and Niebuhrs, with its renewed interest in original sin and impossible ethical ideals, there will also be readers who will be excited by this little volume precisely because it does ethics in the context of such neofundamentalist doctrines. These readers will find here a forceful statement of an ethics which not only has affinities to religious views to which they are already inclined, but which is superior in clarity and in reasoning to those which are offered by more recent writers of a similar bent of mind.

To still a third sort of reader Edwards' book will be interesting as an item of intellectual history. He will find here not only Calvinism but a novel form of Christian ethics, a profound restatement of the New Testament law of love in terms borrowed from the metaphysics of the Platonists, on the one hand, and from the moral aestheticism and sentimentalism of Shaftesbury and Hutcheson, on the other. He will also find an interesting treatment of the claims of those, like Samuel Clarke and Joseph Butler, who refused to identify virtue with benevolence, and preferred to identify it with a conformity to the fitnesses, relations, and proportions of things, or to the dictates of conscience or a moral sense. He may even wonder whether Edwards had read Butler's *Sermons* and *Dissertation on Virtue*, so striking are the similarities and the differences between the two authors. And, should he move from the question of its origins to that of its influences, he would learn that Edwards' essay was the beginning of a tradition of teleological and utilitarian thinking which strongly opposed the deontological intuitionism prevailing in American ethics in the nineteenth century. For over a hundred years the Edwardian ethics was stated and restated by such men as Samuel Hopkins, Joseph Bellamy, Timothy Dwight, N. W. Taylor, C. G. Finney, Mark Hopkins, and J. H. Fairchild. Through them Edwards may have been at least partly responsible for the textbook vogue enjoyed in the early 1800's by William Paley's utilitarian *Principles of Moral and Political Philosophy,* and for the eventual triumph of teleological ethics at the opening of the present century.

Even the most up-to-date of contemporary moral philosophers will find something of interest in Edwards' book. For example, in Chapter VIII Edwards seems to take an emotivist view of moral judgments, but argues that they are not therefore arbitrary or without foundation in the nature of things; and what he says in making this out, though somewhat curious, is also very suggestive. Likewise intriguing is his discussion of the love of consistency or what is known in the latest circles as the universalization requirement with respect to moral judgments.

Edwards' views on the nature of virtue may be summarized as follows. As indicated earlier, he sides with those who hold that moral judgments, approvals and disapprovals, are "founded in sentiment, and not in reason." ". . . sentiment among mankind is the rule

of language, as to what is called by the name of good
and evil . . ." He identifies the "sense" involved with
a sense of beauty, that is, a sense by which we "immediately perceive pleasure in the presence" of certain
kinds of things, for, he argues, virtue is a certain species of beauty, namely, beauty of heart. But there are
for him two kinds of beauty of disposition and action,
and two distinct senses by which they are "relished."
The one beauty consists in benevolence or love of
Being in general, the other in harmony, proportion, or
uniformity in variety. The former is primary, highest,
true, spiritual, divine beauty, and is relished by a spiritual or divine sense; the other is a secondary, inferior,
natural beauty, and is perceived by a "fleshly," natural sense. True virtue, then, is beauty of the first
kind, or "consent and good will to Being in general."
Beauty of heart and action of the second kind is also
a form of excellence, but an inferior one, and it is not
true virtue. Hence there are two kinds or levels of
morality, a true or spiritual morality and a natural or
inferior one, and there are two sources of morality, as
Bergson calls them, both planted in us by God, by
whom they are generated.

The two moralities, however, are not discrepant in
content. Nothing is approved by the one sense which
will not also be approved, though from a different per-
spective, by the other. ". . . natural conscience, if the
understanding be properly enlightened, . . . concurs
with the law of God, and is of equal extent with it,
and joins its voice with it in every article." Only the

perspectives are different—the natural conscience does not speak out of a relish of the true beauty of benevolence to Being in general.

True virtue, accordingly, is love of Being in general, or rather, love of intelligent Being in general, for "Beings that have no perception or will . . . are not properly capable objects of benevolence." This means loving all intelligent Beings in proportion to their dignity, that is, in proportion to their degree of existence and to the degree of their own love of Being as such. But God is infinite in both respects, and hence true virtue is primarily love of God. Love of neighbor is true virtue only if it proceeds from a love of Being as such which is primarily directed at God. Those theistic moralists who slight this truth are simply not taking God seriously. Loving a Being means, in general, seeking to promote his happiness if it is not yet complete, rejoicing in it in so far as he already has it, and delighting in such beauty as he may have. Love of God must consist mainly in rejoicing in and glorifying Him, love of a creature mainly in seeking his good, which is knowledge of God's glory and beauty, union with God, conformity to Him, love to Him, and joy in Him.

In the inferior morality of natural man the main element is the sense of justice, as deontological intuitionists have always stressed, that is, the sense that certain actions are fitting or unfitting in certain situations or relations (for example, in relation to parents, to husband, or to God). But since the motive here is "a relish of uniformity and proportion," this natural justice involves no true virtue. Augustine would have called it a splendid vice. Moreover, this sense of justice is combined in our common morality with a natural love of consistency, which is a virtual third source of moral or quasi-moral judgments, leading us to be uneasy if we do to others what we would not want them to do to us. This love of consistency, which explains so much of our "reflection of conscience," arises from "an inclination to feel and act as one with ourselves" and so stems from self-love, which, of course, is even farther from true virtue than the sense of justice.

In this essay Edwards does not subscribe to a wholly egoistic theory of the psychology of natural man, as he has been said to do, and in fact seems to do in other writings. He is very acute, it is true, in arguing that a great deal of our natural morality and so-called virtue may be derived from self-love. His main concern, however, is merely to show that nothing but what proceeds from a genuine benevolence to Being (or love of God) has any true virtue in it—that all of what we naturally regard as moral and good arises either from self-love, from the sense of justice (inferior beauty), or at best from limited altruistic impulses which do not incorporate a full benevolence of spirit, and hence is none of it true virtue.

For the rest of Edwards' relevant views we must look to other writings. In them he tells us that, since the Fall, no man is born with either the sense of true virtue or the love of Being in general. Nor can any man acquire them by his own effort or that of his fellows. Man is naturally incapable of true virtue. He ought to love, but he cannot. In fact, for all his natural morality, he is corrupt and vicious. Yet he is not without hope. For those who are elect, there is the grace of God through which is planted in them the seed of true benevolence by the regenerating work of the Holy Spirit. The others, however, are without excuse for their sin, for they have the testimony of their natural conscience; their actions are indeed predestined, but they may nevertheless be held subject to moral judgment, and hence to reward and punishment.

That right or virtuous conduct is benevolent or loving conduct, conduct which is aimed at the general well-being, is a widely accepted view—Christians, religious liberals, pragmatists, and utilitarians all alike subscribe to it in one form or another. Except among orthodox Christians, however, it has been accompanied by two assumptions: that men are naturally capable of a considerable measure of this benevolent concern for being in general, and that our prevailing moral judgments in fact embody such a benevolence or can be made to do so by a process of education. These assumptions Edwards challenged with particular force. Some of those who question these assumptions, however, have drawn the conclusion that morality must be identified either with a policy of enlightened self-interest or with a search for balance, harmony, pattern, or proportion in the conduct of

life. Such conclusions Edwards resolutely refused to
draw. He held to his high ideal of true virtue, and
argued instead that there is a grace whereby some
may be enabled to attain it. It does not come to all,
but no one can honestly say, "It will not come to me,"
for if he is genuinely concerned, then it has already
come.

CONTENTS

CHAPTER I

Showing Wherein the Essence of True Virtue Consists

WHATEVER controversies and variety of opinions there are about the nature of virtue, yet all excepting some sceptics, who deny any real difference between virtue and vice, mean by it something beautiful, or rather some kind of beauty or excellency. It is not all beauty that is called virtue; for instance, not the beauty of a building, of a flower, or of the rainbow; but some beauty belonging to beings that have perception and will. It is not all beauty of mankind that is called virtue; for instance, not the external beauty of the countenance or shape, gracefulness of motion, or harmony of voice: but it is a beauty that has its original seat in the mind. But yet perhaps not every thing that may be called a beauty of mind, is properly called virtue. There is a beauty of understanding and speculation; there is something in the ideas and conceptions of great philosophers and statesmen, that may be called beautiful: which is a different thing from what is most commonly meant by virtue.

But virtue is the beauty of those qualities and acts of the mind that are of a moral nature, i.e. such as are attended with desert or worthiness of praise or blame.

Things of this sort it is generally agreed, so far as I know, do not belong merely to speculation: but to the disposition and will, or (to use a general word I suppose commonly well understood) to the heart. Therefore I suppose I shall not depart from the common opinion when I say, that virtue is the beauty of the qualities and exercises of the heart, or those actions which proceed from them. So that when it is enquired, what is the nature of true virtue? This is the same as to enquire what that is, which renders any habit, disposition, or exercise of the heart truly beautiful?

I use the phrase true virtue, and speak of things truly beautiful, because I suppose it will generally be allowed, that there is a distinction to be made between some things which are truly virtuous, and others which only seem to be so, through a partial and imperfect view of things: that some actions and dispositions appear beautiful, if considered partially and superficially, or with regard to some things belonging to them, and in some of their circumstances and tendencies, which would appear otherwise in a more extensive and comprehensive view, wherein they are seen clearly in their whole nature, and the extent of their connections in the universality of things.

There is a general and particular beauty. By a particular beauty, I mean that by which a thing appears beautiful when considered only with regard to its connection with, and tendency to, some particular things within a limited, and as it were a private sphere. And a general beauty is that by which a thing appears beautiful when viewed most perfectly, comprehensively and universally, with regard to all its tendencies, and its connections with every thing to which it stands related. The former may be without and against the latter. As a few notes in a tune, taken only by themselves and in their relation to one another, may be harmonious, which, when considered with respect to all the notes in the tune, or the entire series of sounds they are connected with, may be very discordant, and disagreeable. That only, therefore, is what I mean by true virtue, which, belonging to the heart of an intelligent being, is beautiful by a general beauty, or beautiful in a comprehensive view, as it is in itself, and as related to every thing with which it stands connected. And therefore, when we are enquiring concerning the nature of true virtue—wherein this true and general beauty of the heart does most essentially consist—this is my answer to the enquiry:

True virtue most essentially consists in *benevolence to being in general.* Or perhaps, to speak more accurately, it is that consent, propensity and union of heart to being in general, which is immediately exercised in a general good will.

The things before observed respecting the nature of true virtue, naturally lead us to such a notion of it. If it has its seat in the heart, and is the general goodness and beauty of the disposition and its exercise, in the most comprehensive view, considered with regard to its universal tendency, and as related to every thing with which it stands connected; what can it consist in, but a consent and good will to being in general? Beauty does not consist in discord and dissent, but in consent and agreement. And if every intelligent being is some way related to being in general, and is a part of the universal system of existence; and so stands in connection with the whole; what can its general and true beauty be, but its union and consent with the great whole?

If any such thing can be supposed as an union of heart to some particular being, or number of beings, disposing it to benevolence to a private circle or system of beings, which are but a small part of the whole; not implying a tendency to an union with the great system, and not at all inconsistent with enmity towards being in general, this I suppose not to be of the nature of true virtue; although it may in some respects be good, and may appear beautiful in a confined and contracted view of things. But of this more afterwards.

It is abundantly plain by the holy scriptures, and generally allowed, not only by Christian divines, but by the more considerable Deists, that virtue most essentially consists in love. And I suppose it is owned by the most considerable writers, to consist in general love of benevolence, or kind affection: though it seems to me the meaning of some in this affair is not sufficiently explained; which perhaps occasions some error or confusion in discourses on this subject.

When I say true virtue consists in love to being in general, I shall not be likely to be understood, that no one act of the mind or exercise of love is of the nature of true virtue, but what has being in general, or the great system of universal existence, for its direct and immediate object: so that no exercise of love, or kind affection to any one particular being, that is but a small part of this whole, has any thing of the nature of true virtue. But that the nature of true virtue consists in a disposition to benevolence towards being in general; though from such a disposition may arise exercises of love to particular beings, as objects are presented and occasions arise. No wonder that he who is of a generally benevolent disposition, should be more disposed than another to have his heart moved with benevolent affection to particular persons, with whom he is acquainted and conversant, and from whom arise the greatest and most frequent occasions for exciting his benevolent temper. But my meaning is, that no affections towards particular persons or beings are of the nature of true virtue, but such as arise from a generally benevolent temper, or from that habit or frame of mind, wherein consists a disposition to love being in general.

And perhaps it is needless for me to give notice to my readers, that when I speak of an intelligent being having a heart united and benevolently disposed to being in general, I thereby mean intelligent being in general. Not inanimate things, or beings that have no perception or will; which are not properly capable objects of benevolence.

Love is commonly distinguished into love of benevolence, and love of complacence. Love of benevolence is that affection or propensity of the heart to any being, which causes it to incline to its well-being, or disposes it to desire and take pleasure in its happiness. And if I mistake not, it is agreeable to the common opinion, that beauty in the object is not always the ground of this propensity; but that there may be a disposition to the welfare of those that are not considered as beautiful, unless mere existence be accounted a beauty. And benevolence or goodness in the divine Being is generally supposed, not only to be prior to the beauty of many of its objects, but to their existence; so as to be the ground both of their existence and their beauty, rather than the foundation of God's benevolence; as it is supposed that it is God's goodness which moved him to give them both being and beauty. So that if all virtue primarily consists in that affection of heart to being, which is exercised in benevolence, or an inclination to its good, then God's virtue is so extended as to include a propensity not only to being actually existing, and actually beautiful, but to possible being, so as to incline him to give a being beauty and happiness.

What is commonly called love of complacence, presupposes beauty. For it is no other than delight in beauty; or complacence in the person or being beloved for his beauty. If virtue be the beauty of an intelligent being, and virtue consists in love, then it is a plain inconsistence, to suppose that virtue primarily consists in any love to its object for its beauty; either in a love of complacence, which is delight in a being for his beauty, or in a love of benevolence, that has the beauty of its object for its foundation. For that would be to suppose, that the beauty of intelligent beings primarily consists in love to beauty; or that their virtue first of all consists in their love to virtue. Which is an inconsistence, and going in a circle. Because it makes virtue, or beauty of mind, the foundation or first motive of that love wherein virtue originally consists, or wherein the very first virtue consists; or, it supposes the first virtue to be the consequence and effect of virtue. Which makes the first virtue both the ground and the consequence, both cause and effect of itself. Doubtless virtue primarily consists in something else besides any effect or consequence of virtue. If virtue consists primarily in love to virtue, then virtue, the thing loved, is the love of virtue: so that virtue must consist in the love of the love of virtue—and so on in infinitum. For there is no end of going back in a circle. We never come to any beginning or foundation; it is without beginning, and hangs on nothing. Therefore, if the essence of virtue, or beauty of mind, lies in love, or a disposition to love, it must primarily consist in something different both from complacence, which is a delight in beauty, and also from any benevolence that has the beauty of its object for its foundation. Because it is absurd to say, that virtue is primarily and first of all the consequence of itself; which makes virtue primarily prior to itself.

Nor can virtue primarily consist in gratitude; or one

being's benevolence to another for his benevolence to him. Because this implies the same inconsistence. For it supposes a benevolence prior to gratitude, which is the cause of gratitude. The first benevolence cannot be gratitude. Therefore there is room left for no other conclusion, than that the primary object of virtuous love is being, simply considered; or that true virtue primarily consists, not in love to any particular beings, because of their virtue or beauty, nor in gratitude, because they love us; but in a propensity and union of heart to being simply considered; exciting absolute benevolence, if I may so call it, to being in general. I say true virtue primarily consists in this. For I am far from asserting, that there is no true virtue in any other love than this absolute benevolence. But I would express what appears to me to be the truth on this subject, in the following particulars.

The first object of a virtuous benevolence is being, simply considered; and if being, simply considered, be its object, then being in general is its object; and what it has an ultimate propensity to is the highest good of being in general. And it will seek the good of every individual being unless it be conceived as not consistent with the highest good of being in general. In which case the good of a particular being, or some beings, may be given up for the sake of the highest good of being in general. And particularly, if there be any being statedly and irreclaimably opposite, and an enemy to being in general, then consent and adherence to being in general will induce the truly virtuous heart to forsake that enemy, and to oppose it.

Further, if *being*, simply considered, be the first object of a truly virtuous benevolence, then that object who has most of being, or has the greatest share of existence, other things being equal, so far as such a being is exhibited to our faculties, will have the greatest share of the propensity and benevolent affections of the heart. I say, "other things being equal," especially because there is a secondary object of virtuous benevolence, that I shall take notice of presently, which must be considered as the ground or motive to a purely virtuous benevolence. Pure benevolence in its first exercise is nothing else but being's uniting consent, or propensity to being; and inclining to the general highest good, and to each being, whose welfare is consistent with the highest general good, in proportion to the degree of existence,* understand, "other things being equal."

The second object of a virtuous propensity of heart is benevolent being. A secondary ground of pure benevolence is virtuous benevolence itself in its object.

* I say, "in proportion to the degree of existence," because one being may have more existence than another, as he may be greater than another. That which is great has more existence, and is further from nothing, than that which is little. One being may have every thing positive belonging to it, or every thing which goes to its positive existence (in opposition to defect) in an higher degree than another; or a greater capacity and power, greater understanding, every faculty and every positive quality in a higher degree. An archangel must be supposed to have more existence, and to be every way further removed from nonentity, than a worm.

When any one under the influence of general benevolence, sees another being possessed of the like general
benevolence, this attaches his heart to him, and draws
forth greater love to him, than merely his having
existence: because so far as the being beloved has
love to being in general, so far his own being is, as it
were, enlarged; extends to, and in some sort compre-
hends being in general: and therefore, he that is governed by love to being in general, must of necessity
have complacence in him, and the greater degree of
benevolence to him, as it were out of gratitude to him
for his love to general existence, that his own heart is
extended and united to, and so looks on its interest
as its own. It is because his heart is thus united to
being in general, that he looks on a benevolent propensity to being in general, wherever he sees it, as the
beauty of the being in whom it is; an excellency that
renders him worthy of esteem, complacence, and the
greater good-will. But several things may be noted
more particularly concerning this secondary ground
of a truly virtuous love.

1. That loving a being on this ground necessarily
arises from pure benevolence to being in general, and
comes to the same thing. For he that has a simple and
pure good will to general existence, must love that
temper in others, that agrees and conspires with itself.
A spirit of consent to being must agree with consent to being. That which truly and sincerely seeks
the good of others, must approve of, and love that

which joins with him in seeking the good of others.

2. This secondary ground of virtuous love is the thing wherein true moral or spiritual beauty primarily consists. Yea, spiritual beauty consists wholly in this, and in the various qualities and exercises of mind which proceed from it, and the external actions which proceed from these internal qualities and exercises. And in these things consists all true virtue, viz. in this love of being, and the qualities and acts which arise from it.

3. As all spiritual beauty lies in these virtuous principles and acts, so it is primarily on this account they are beautiful, viz. that they imply consent and union with being in general. This is the primary and most essential beauty of every thing that can justly be called by the name of virtue, or is any moral excellency in the eye of one who has a perfect view of things. I say, "the primary and most essential beauty," because there is a secondary and inferior sort of beauty; which I shall take notice of afterwards.

4. This spiritual beauty, which is but a secondary ground of virtuous benevolence, is the ground not only of benevolence, but complacence, and is the primary ground of the latter; that is, when the complacence is truly virtuous. Love to us in particular, and kindness received may be a secondary ground: but this is the primary objective foundation of it.

5. It must be noted, that the degree of the amiableness of true virtue primarily consisting in consent, and

a benevolent propensity of heart to being in general, is not in the simple proportion of the degree of benevolent affection seen, but in a proportion compounded of the greatness of the benevolent being, or the degree of being and the degree of benevolence. One who loves being in general, will necessarily value good will to being in general, wherever he sees it. But if he sees the same benevolence in two beings, he will value it more in two, than in one only. Because it is a greater thing, more favourable to being in general, to have two beings to favour it, than only one of them. For there is more being that favours being: both together having more being than one alone. So if one being be as great as two, has as much existence as both together, and has the same degree of general benevolence, it is more favourable to being in general, than if there were general benevolence in a being that had but half that share of existence. As a large quantity of gold, with the same quality, is more valuable than a small quantity of the same metal.

6. It is impossible that any one should truly relish this beauty, consisting in general benevolence, who has not that temper himself. I have observed, that if any being is possessed of such a temper, he will unavoidably be pleased with the same temper in another. And it may in like manner be demonstrated, that it is such a spirit, and nothing else, which will relish such a spirit. For if a being destitute of benevolence, should love benevolence to being in general, it

would prize and seek that for which it had no value. For how should one love and value a disposition to a thing, or a tendency to promote it, and for that very reason, when the thing itself is what he is regardless of, and has no value for, nor desires to have promoted.

CHAPTER II

Showing How That Love, Wherein True Virtue Consists, Respects the Divine Being and Created Things

FROM what has been said, it is evident, that true virtue must chiefly consist in *love to God;* the Being of beings, infinitely the greatest and best. This appears, whether we consider the primary or secondary ground of virtuous love. It was observed that the first objective ground of that love wherein true virtue consists, is *being* simply considered: and, as a necessary consequence of this, that being who has the greatest share of universal existence has proportionably the greatest share of virtuous benevolence, so far as such a being is exhibited to the faculties of our minds, other things being equal. But God has infinitely the greatest share of existence. So that all other being, even the whole universe, is as nothing in comparison of the divine Being.

And if we consider the secondary ground of love, or moral excellency, the same thing will appear. For as God is infinitely the greatest Being, so he is allowed to be infinitely the most beautiful and excellent: and all the beauty to be found throughout the whole creation, is but the reflection of the diffused beams of that Being who hath an infinite fulness of brightness and

glory. God's beauty is infinitely more valuable than
that of all other beings upon both those accounts
mentioned, viz. the degree of his virtue and the greatness of his being, possessed of this virtue. And God
has sufficiently exhibited himself, both in his being,
and his infinite greatness and excellency: and has
given us faculties, whereby we are capable of plainly
discovering his immense superiority to all other beings in these respects. Therefore he that has true virtue, consisting in benevolence to being in general, and
in benevolence to virtuous being, must necessarily
have a supreme love to God, both of benevolence
and complacence. And all true virtue must radically
and essentially, and as it were summarily consist in
this. Because God is not only infinitely greater and
more excellent than all other being, but he is the head
of the universal system of existence; the foundation
and fountain of all being and all beauty; from whom
all is perfectly derived, and on whom all is most absolutely and perfectly dependent; of whom, and through
whom, and to whom is all being and all perfection;
and whose being and beauty are, as it were, the sum
and comprehension of all existence and excellence:
much more than the sun is the fountain and summary
comprehension of all the light and brightness of the
day.

If it should be objected, that virtue consists primarily in benevolence, but that our fellow-creatures,
and not God, seem to be the most proper objects of
our benevolence; inasmuch as our goodness extendeth

not to God, and we cannot be profitable to him. To
this I answer,

1. A benevolent propensity of heart is exercised,
not only in seeking to promote the happiness of the
being towards whom it is exercised, but also in rejoicing in his happiness. Even as gratitude for benefits
received will not only excite endeavours to requite the
kindness we receive, by equally benefiting our benefactor, but also if he be above any need of us, or we
have nothing to bestow, and are unable to repay his
kindness, it will dispose us to rejoice in his prosperity.

2. Though we are not able to give any thing to
God, which we have of our own independently; yet
we may be the instruments of promoting his glory, in
which he takes a true and proper delight.* Whatever
influence such an objection may seem to have on the
minds of some, yet is there any that owns the being of
a God, who will deny that any benevolent affection is
due to God, and proper to be exercised towards him?
If no benevolence is to be exercised towards God,
because we cannot profit him, then for the same reason, neither is gratitude to be exercised towards him
for his benefits to us: because we cannot requite him.
But where is the man who believes a God and a
providence, that will say this?

There seems to be an inconsistence in some writers
on morality, in this respect, that they do not wholly

---

*As was shown at large in the former treatise, on God's end
in creating the world, Chap. I, sect. 4, whither I must refer
the reader for a more full answer to this objection.

exclude a regard to the Deity out of their schemes
of morality, but yet mention it so slightly, that they
leave me room and reason to suspect they esteem it a
less important and a subordinate part of true morality: and insist on benevolence to the created system,
in such a manner as would naturally lead one to suppose they look upon that as by far the most important
and essential thing in their scheme. But why should
this be? If true virtue consists partly in a respect to
God, then doubtless it consists chiefly in it. If true
morality requires that we should have some regard,
some benevolent affection to our Creator, as well as
to his creatures, then doubtless it requires the first
regard to be paid to him; and that he be every way
the supreme object of our benevolence. If his being
above our reach, and beyond all capacity of being
profited by us, does not hinder but that nevertheless
he is the proper object of our love, then it does not
hinder that he should be loved according to his dignity, or according to the degree in which he has those
things wherein worthiness of regard consists, so far
as we are capable of it. But this worthiness, none will
deny, consists in these two things, greatness and moral
goodness. And those that own a God, do not deny
that he infinitely exceeds all other beings in these. If
the Deity is to be looked upon as within that system
of beings which properly terminates our benevolence,
or belonging to that whole, certainly he is to be regarded as the head of the system, and the chief part
of it; if it be proper to call him a part, who is infinitely

more than all the rest, and in comparison of whom, and without whom all the rest are nothing, either as to beauty or existence. And therefore certainly, unless we will be Atheists, we must allow that true virtue does primarily and most essentially consist in a supreme love to God; and that where this is wanting, there can be no true virtue.

But this being a matter of the highest importance, I shall say something further to make it plain that love to God is most essential to true virtue; and that no benevolence whatsoever to other beings can be of the nature of true virtue without it.

And therefore, let it be supposed that some beings, by natural instinct or by some other means, have a determination of mind to union and benevolence to a particular person, or private system,* which is but a small part of the universal system of being: and that this disposition or determination of mind is independent on, or not subordinate to benevolence to being in general. Such a determination, disposition, or affection of mind is not of the nature of true virtue.

* It may be here noted, that when hereafter I use such a phrase as private system of being, or others similar, I thereby intend any system or society of beings that contains but a small part of the great system, comprehending the universality of existence. I think that may well be called a private system, which is but an infinitely small part of this great whole we stand related to. I therefore also call that affection private affection, which is limited to so narrow a circle: and that general affection or benevolence, which has being in general for its object.

This is allowed by all with regard to self-love; in which good will is confined to one single person only. And there are the same reasons why any other private affection or good will, though extending to a society of persons independent of, and unsubordinate to, benevolence to the universality, should not be esteemed truly virtuous. For notwithstanding it extends to a number of persons, which taken together are more than a single person, yet the whole falls infinitely short of the universality of existence; and if put in the scales with it, has no greater proportion to it than a single person.

However, it may not be amiss more particularly to consider the reasons why private affections, or good will limited to a particular circle of beings, falling infinitely short of the whole existence, and not dependent upon it, nor subordinate to general benevolence, cannot be of the nature of true virtue.

1. Such a private affection, detached from general benevolence, and independent on it, as the case may be, will be against general benevolence, or of a contrary tendency; and will set a person against general existence, and make him an enemy to it. As it is with selfishness, or when a man is governed by a regard to his own private interest; independent of regard to the public good, such a temper exposes a man to act the part of an enemy to the public. As in every case wherein his private interest seems to clash with the public; or in all those cases wherein such things are presented to his view, that suit his personal appetites

or private inclinations, but are inconsistent with the good of the public. On which account a selfish, contracted, narrow spirit is generally abhorred, and is esteemed base and sordid. But if a man's affection takes in half a dozen more, and his regards extend so far beyond his own single person as to take in his children and family; or if it reaches further still to a larger circle, but falls infinitely short of the universal system, and is exclusive of being in general; his private affection exposes him to the same thing, viz. to pursue the interest of its particular object in opposition to general existence: which is certainly contrary to the tendency of true virtue; yea directly contrary to the main and most essential thing in its nature, the thing on account of which chiefly its nature and tendency is good. For the chief and most essential good that is in virtue, is its favouring being in general. Now certainly, if private affection to a limited system had in itself the essential nature of virtue, it would be impossible that it should in any circumstance whatsoever, have a tendency and inclination directly contrary to that wherein the essence of virtue chiefly consists.

2. Private affection, if not subordinate to general affection, is not only liable, as the case may be, to issue in enmity to being in general, but has a tendency to it as the case certainly is, and must necessarily be. For he that is influenced by private affection, not subordinate to a regard to being in general, sets up its particular or limited object above being in general;

and this most naturally tends to enmity against the latter, which is by right the great supreme, ruling, and absolutely sovereign object of our regard. Even as the setting up another prince as supreme in any kingdom, distinct from the lawful sovereign, naturally tends to enmity against the lawful sovereign. Wherever it is sufficiently published, that the supreme, infinite, and all-comprehending Being requires a supreme regard to himself; and insists upon it, that our respect to him should universally rule in our hearts, and every other affection be subordinate to it, and this under the pain of his displeasure (as we must suppose it is in the world of intelligent creatures, if God maintains a moral kingdom in the world), then a consciousness of our having chosen and set up another prince to rule over us, and subjected our hearts to him, and continuing in such an act, must unavoidably excite enmity, and fix us in a stated opposition to the supreme Being. This demonstrates, that affection to a private society or system, independent on general benevolence, cannot be of the nature of true virtue. For this would be absurd, that it has the nature and essence of true virtue, and yet at the same time has a tendency opposite to true virtue.

3. Not only would affection to a private system, unsubordinate to a regard to being in general, have a tendency to oppose the supreme object of virtuous affection, as its effect and consequence, but would become itself an opposition to that object. Considered by itself in its nature, detached from its effects, it is

an instance of great opposition to the rightful supreme object of our respect. For it exalts its private object above the other great and infinite object; and sets that up as supreme in opposition to this. It puts down being in general, which is infinitely superior in itself and infinitely more important, in an inferior place; yea, subjects the supreme general object to this private infinitely inferior object: which is to treat it with great contempt, and truly to act in opposition to it, and to act in opposition to the true order of things, and in opposition to that which is infinitely the supreme interest; making this supreme and infinitely important interest, as far as in us lies, to be subject to, and dependent on an interest infinitely inferior. This is to act the part of an enemy to it. He that takes a subject and exalts him above his prince, sets him as supreme instead of the prince, and treats his prince wholly as a subject, therein acts the part of an enemy to his prince.

From these things I think it is manifest, that no affection limited to any private system, not dependent on, nor subordinate to being in general, can be of the nature of true virtue; and this, whatever the private system be, let it be more or less extensive, consisting of a greater or smaller number of individuals, so long as it contains an infinitely little part of universal existence, and so bears no proportion to the great all-comprehending system. And consequently, that no affection whatsoever to any creature, or any system of created beings, which is not dependent on, nor subordinate to a propensity or union of the heart to God, the supreme and infinite Being can be of the nature of true virtue.

From hence also it is evident, that the divine virtue, or the virtue of the divine mind, must consist primarily in love to himself, or in the mutual love and friendship which subsists eternally and necessarily between the several persons in the Godhead, or that infinitely strong propensity there is in these divine persons one to another. There is no need of multiplying words to prove that it must be thus, on a supposition that virtue, in its most essential nature, consists in benevolent affection or propensity of heart towards being in general; and so flowing out to particular beings in a greater or lesser degree, according to the measure of existence and beauty which they are possessed of. It will also follow from the foregoing things, that God's goodness and love to created beings is derived from, and subordinate to his love to himself.*

With respect to the manner in which a virtuous love in created beings, one to another, is dependent on, and derived from love to God, this will appear by a proper consideration of what has been said; that it is sufficient to render love to any created being virtuous, if it arise from the temper of mind wherein consists a disposition to love God supremely. Because

* In what manner it is so, I have endeavoured in some measure to explain in the preceding discourse of God's end in creating the world.

it appears from what has been already observed, all
that love to particular beings, which is the fruit of a
benevolent propensity of heart to being in general, is
virtuous love. But, as has been remarked, a benevolent propensity of heart to being in general, and a
temper or disposition to love God supremely, are in
effect the same thing. Therefore, if love to a created
being comes from that temper or propensity of the
heart, it is virtuous. However, every particular exercise of love to a creature may not sensibly arise from
any exercise of love to God, or an explicit consideration of any similitude, conformity, union or relation
to God, in the creature beloved.

The most proper evidence of love to a created being arising from that temper of mind wherein consists
a supreme propensity of heart to God, seems to be
the agreeableness of the kind and degree of our love
to God's end in our creation, and in the creation of
all things, and the coincidence of the exercise of our
love, in their manner, order, and measure, with the
manner in which God himself exercises love to the
creature in the creation and government of the world,
and the way in which God, as the first cause and
supreme disposer of all things, has respect to the
creature's happiness in subordination to himself as his
own supreme end. For the true virtue of created beings is doubtless their highest excellency, and their
true goodness, and that by which they are especially
agreeable to the mind of their Creator. But the true
goodness of a thing must be its agreeableness to its

end, or its fitness to answer the design for which it was made. Therefore they are good moral agents, whose temper of mind or propensity of heart, is agreeable to the end for which God made moral agents. But as has been shown, the last end for which God has made moral agents must be the last end for which God has made all things: it being evident, that the moral world is the end of the rest of the world; the inanimate and unintelligent world being made for the rational and moral world, as much as a house is prepared for the inhabitants.

By these things it appears, that a truly virtuous mind, being as it were under the sovereign dominion of love to God, above all things, seeks the glory of God, and makes this his supreme, governing, and ultimate end. This consists in the expression of God's perfections in their proper effects, the manifestation of God's glory to created understandings, the communications of the infinite fulness of God to the creature—the creature's highest esteem of God, love to, and joy in him—and in the proper exercises and expressions of these. And so far as a virtuous mind exercises true virtue in benevolence to created beings, it chiefly seeks the good of the creature; consisting in its knowledge or view of God's glory and beauty, its union with God, conformity and love to him, and joy in him. And that disposition of heart, that consent, union, or propensity of mind to being in general, which appears chiefly in such exercises, is *virtue*, truly so called; or in other words, true *grace* and real *holiness.* And no other disposition or affection but this is of the nature of virtue.

COROLLARY. Hence it appears that those schemes of religion or moral philosophy, which—however well in some respects they may treat of benevolence to mankind and other virtues depending on it, yet—have not a supreme regard to God, and love to him laid as the foundation, and all other virtues handled in a connection with this, and in subordination to it, are not true schemes of philosophy, but are fundamentally and essentially defective. And whatever other benevolence or generosity towards mankind, and other virtues, or moral qualifications which go by that name, any are possessed of, that are not attended with a love to God which is altogether above them, and to which they are subordinate, and on which they are dependent, there is nothing of the nature of true virtue or religion in them. And it may be asserted in general, that nothing is of the nature of true virtue, in which God is not the first and the last; or which, with regard to their exercises in general, have not their first foundation and source in apprehensions of God's supreme dignity and glory, and in answerable esteem and love of him, and have not respect to God as the supreme end.

CHAPTER III

Concerning the Secondary and Inferior Kind of Beauty

THOUGH what has been spoken of is alone justly esteemed the true beauty of moral agents, or spiritual beings; this alone being what would appear beautiful in them upon a clear and comprehensive view of things; and therefore alone is the moral amiableness of beings that have understanding and will, in the eyes of him that perfectly sees all things as they are; yet there are other qualities, other sensations, propensities and affections of mind, and principles of action, that often obtain the epithet of virtuous, and by many are supposed to have the nature of true virtue, which are entirely of a distinct nature from this, and have nothing of that kind; and therefore are erroneously confounded with real virtue.

That consent, agreement, or union of being to being, which has been spoken of, viz. the union or propensity of minds to mental or spiritual existence, may be called the highest and primary beauty; being the proper and peculiar beauty of spiritual and moral beings, which are the highest and first part of the universal system, for whose sake all the rest has existence. Yet there is another, inferior, secondary beauty, which is some image of this, and which is not peculiar to spiritual beings, but is found even in inanimate things; which consists in a mutual consent and agreement of different things, in form, manner, quantity, and visible end or design; called by the various names of regularity, order, uniformity, symmetry, proportion, harmony, etc. Such is the mutual agreement of the various sides of a square, or equilateral triangle, or of a regular polygon. Such is, as it were, the mutual consent of the different parts of the periphery of a circle, or surface of a sphere, and of the corresponding parts of an ellipsis. Such is the agreement of the colors, figures, dimensions, and distances of the different spots on a chess board. Such is the beauty of the figures on a piece of chintz or brocade. Such is the beautiful proportion of the various parts of a human body or countenance. And such is the sweet mutual consent and agreement of the various notes of a melodious tune. This is the same that Mr. Hutchinson, in his Treatise on Beauty, expresses by uniformity in the midst of variety. Which is no other than the consent or agreement of different things in form, quantity, etc. He observes, that the greater the variety is in equal uniformity the greater the beauty. Which is no more than to say, the more there are of different mutually agreeing things, the greater is the beauty. And the reason of that is, because it is more considerable to have many things consent one with another, than a few only.

The beauty which consists in the visible fitness of

a thing to its use, and unity of design, is not a distinct sort of beauty from this. For it is to be observed, that one thing which contributes to the beauty of the agreement and proportion of various things, is their relation one to another; which connects them, and introduces them together into view and consideration, and whereby one suggests the other to the mind, and the mind is led to compare them, and so to expect and desire agreement. Thus the uniformity of two or more pillars, as they may happen to be found in different places, is not an equal degree of beauty, as that uniformity in so many pillars in the corresponding parts of the same building. So means and an intended effect are related one to another. The answerableness of a thing to its use is only the proportion and fitness of a cause or means to a visibly designed effect, and so an effect suggested to the mind by the idea of the means. This kind of beauty is not entirely different from that beauty which there is in fitting a mortice to its tenon. Only when the beauty consists in unity of design, or the adaptness of a variety of things to promote one intended effect, in which all conspire, as the various parts of an ingenious complicated machine, there is a double beauty, as there is a twofold agreement and conformity. First, there is the agreement of the various parts to the designed end. Secondly, through this designed end or effect, all the various particulars agree one with another as the general medium of their union, whereby they, being united in this third, are all united one to another.

The reason, or at least one reason, why God has made this kind of mutual agreement of things beautiful and grateful to those intelligent beings that perceive it, probably is, that there is in it some image of the true, spiritual, original beauty which has been spoken of; consisting in being's consent to being, or the union of spiritual beings in a mutual propensity and affection of heart. The other is an image of this, because by that uniformity diverse things become as it were one, as it is in this cordial union. And it pleases God to observe analogy in his works, as is manifest in fact in innumerable instances; and especially to establish inferior things with analogy to superior. Thus, in how many instances has he formed brutes in analogy to the nature of mankind? and plants in analogy to animals, with respect to the manner of their generation, nutrition, etc. And so he has constituted the external world in analogy to the spiritual world in numberless instances; as might be shown, if it were necessary, and here were a proper place for it. Why such analogy in God's works pleased him, it is not needful now to inquire. It is sufficient that he makes an agreement of different things, in their form, manner, measure, etc. to appear beautiful, because here is some image of an higher kind of agreement and consent of spiritual beings. It has pleased him to establish a law of nature, by virtue of which the uniformity and mutual correspondence of a beautiful plant, and the respect which the various parts of a regular building seem to have one to another, and their agreement and union, and the consent or concord of the various notes of a melodious tune, should appear beautiful; because therein is some image of the consent of mind, of the different members of a society or system of intelligent beings, sweetly united in a benevolent agreement of heart.

And here by the way I would further observe, probably it is with regard to this image or resemblance which secondary beauty has of true spiritual beauty, that God has so constituted nature, that the presenting of this inferior beauty, especially in those kinds of it which have the greatest resemblance of the primary beauty, as the harmony of sounds and the beauties of nature, have a tendency to assist those whose hearts are under the influence of a truly virtuous temper to dispose them to the exercises of divine love, and enliven in them a sense of spiritual beauty.

From what has been said we may see that there are two sorts of agreement or consent of one thing to another. (1) There is a cordial agreement; that consists in concord and union of mind and heart: which, if not attended (viewing things in general) with more discord than concord, is true virtue, and the original or primary beauty, which is the only true moral beauty. (2) There is a natural union or agreement; which, though some image of the other, is entirely a distinct thing; the will, disposition, or affection of the heart having no concern in it, but consisting only in uniformity and consent of nature, form, quantity, etc. (as before described), wherein lies an inferior sec-

ondary sort of beauty, which may in distinction from
the other, be called natural beauty. This may be sufficient to let the reader know how I shall hereafter use
the phrase cordial and natural agreement; and moral,
spiritual, divine, and primary original beauty, and
secondary or natural beauty. Concerning this latter,
the inferior kind of beauty, the following things may
be observed:

1. The cause why secondary beauty is grateful to
men, is only a law of nature which God has fixed, or
an instinct he has given to mankind; and not their
perception of the same thing which God is pleased
to regard as the ground or rule by which he has established such a law of nature. This appears in two
things.

(a) That which God respects, as the ground of
this law of nature whereby things have a secondary
beauty are made grateful to men, is their mutual
agreement and proportion, in measure, form, etc. But
in many instances, persons who are gratified and affected with this beauty, do not reflect on that particular agreement and proportion which, according to the
law of nature, is the ground and rule of beauty in the
case, yea, are ignorant of it. Thus a man may be
pleased with the harmony of the notes in a tune, and
yet know nothing of that proportion or adjustment of
the notes, which by the law of nature is the ground
of the melody. He knows not, that the vibrations in
one note regularly coincide with the vibrations in another; that the vibrations of a note coincide in time

with two vibrations of its octave; and that two vibrations of a note coincide with three of its fifth, etc. Yea, he may not know that there are vibrations of the air in the case, or any corresponding motions in the organs of hearing, in the auditory nerve, or animal spirits. So a man may be affected and pleased with a beautiful proportion of the features in a face, and yet not know what that proportion is, or in what measures, quantities, and distances it consists. In this, therefore, a sensation of secondary beauty differs from a sensation of primary and spiritual beauty, consisting in a spiritual union and agreement. What makes the latter grateful, is perceiving the union itself. It is the immediate view of that wherein the beauty fundamentally lies, that is pleasing to the virtuous mind.

(b) God, in establishing such a law—that mutual natural agreement of different things, in form, quantity, etc. should appear beautiful or grateful to men— seems to have had regard to the resemblance there is in such a natural agreement, to that spiritual, cordial agreement, wherein original beauty consists. But it is not any reflection upon, or perception of, such a resemblance, that is the reason why such a form or state of objects appear beautiful to men: but their sensation of pleasure, on a view of this secondary beauty, is immediately owing to the law God has established, or the instinct he has given.

2. Another thing observable concerning this kind of beauty, is that it affects the mind more (other things being equal), when taken notice of in objects

which are of considerable importance, than in little trivial matters. Thus the symmetry of the parts of a human body or countenance, affects the mind more than the beauty of a flower. So the beauty of the solar system, more than as great and as manifold an order and uniformity in a tree. And the proportions of the parts of a church, or a palace, more than the same proportions in some little slight compositions, made to please children.

3. Not only uniformity and proportion, etc. of different things is requisite, in order to this inferior beauty; but also some relation or connection of the things thus agreeing one with another. As the uniformity or likeness of a number of pillars scattered hither and thither, does not constitute beauty, or at least by no means in an equal degree, as uniformity in pillars connected in the same building, in parts that have relation one to another. So if we see things unlike and very disproportioned, in distant places, which have no relation to each other, this excites no such idea of deformity, as disagreement, inequality, or disproportion in things related and connected; and the nearer the relation, and the stricter the connection, so much the greater and more disgustful is the deformity, consisting in their disagreement.

4. This secondary kind of beauty, consisting in uniformity and proportion, not only takes place in material and external things, but also in things immaterial; and is, in very many things, plain and sensible in the latter, as well as the former. And when it is so,

there is no reason why it should not be grateful to them that behold it, in these as well as the other, by virtue of the same sense, or the same determination of mind, to be gratified with uniformity and proportion. If uniformity and proportion be the things that affect and appear agreeable to this sense of beauty, then why should not uniformity and proportion affect the same sense in immaterial things as well as material, if there be equal capacity of discerning it in both? and indeed more in spiritual things (*cœteris paribus*) as these are more important than things merely external and material?

This is not only reasonable to be supposed, but is evident in fact, in numberless instances. There is a beauty of order in society, besides what consists in benevolence, or can be referred to it, which is of the secondary kind. As, when the different members of society have all their appointed office, place and station, according to their several capacities and talents, and every one keeps his place, and continues in his proper business. In this there is a beauty, not of a different kind from the regularity of a beautiful building, or piece of skilful architecture, where the strong pillars are set in their proper place, the pilasters in a place fit for them, the square pieces of marble in the pavement, the panels, partitions, and cornices, etc. in places proper for them. As the agreement of a variety of things in one common design, as of the parts of a building, or complicated machine, is one instance of that regularity which belongs to the secondary kind of beauty, so there is the same kind of beauty in what is called wisdom, consisting in the united tendency of thoughts, ideas and particular volitions, to one general purpose: which is a distinct thing from the goodness of that general purpose, as being useful and benevolent.

There is a beauty in the virtue called justice, which consists in the agreement of different things, that have relation to one another, in nature, manner, and measure; and therefore is the very same sort of beauty with that uniformity and proportion, which is observable in those external and material things that are esteemed beautiful. There is a natural agreement and adaptedness of things that have relation one to another, and a harmonious corresponding of one thing with another. He who from his will does evil to others, should receive evil from the will of him or them whose business it is to take care of the injured, and to act in their behalf, in proportion to the evil of his doings. Things are in natural regularity and mutual agreement, in a literal sense, when he whose heart opposes the general system, should have the hearts of that system, or the heart of the ruler of the system, against him; and, in consequence should receive evil, in proportion to the evil tendency of the opposition of his heart. So there is an agreement in nature and measure, when he that loves has the proper returns of love; when he that from his heart promotes the good of another has his good promoted by the other; for there is a kind of justice in becoming gratitude.

Indeed most of the duties incumbent on us, if well considered, will be found to partake of the nature of justice. There is some natural agreement of one thing to another; some adaptedness of the agent to the object; some answerableness of the act to the occasion; some equality and proportion in things of a similar nature, and of a direct relation one to another. So it is in relative duties; duties of children to parents, and of parents to children; duties of husbands and wives; duties of rulers and subjects; duties of friendship and good neighbourhood; and all duties that we owe to God, our Creator, preserver, and benefactor; and all duties whatsoever, considered as required by God, and as what are to be performed with a regard to Christ.

It is this secondary kind of beauty which Mr. Wollaston seems to have had in his eye when he resolved all virtue into an agreement of inclinations, volitions and actions with truth. He evidently has respect to the justice there is in virtues and duties; which consists in one being expressing such affections, and using such a conduct towards another, as hath a natural agreement and proportion to what is in them, and what we receive from them; which is as much a natural conformity of affection and action with its ground, object, and occasion, as that which is between a true proposition and the thing spoken of in it.

But there is another and higher beauty in true virtue, and in all truly virtuous dispositions and exercises, than what consists in any uniformity or simi-

larity of various things; viz. the union of heart to being
in general, or to God, the being of beings, which
appears in those virtues; and of which those virtues,
when true, are the various expressions or effects. Benevolence to being in general, or to being simply considered, is entirely a distinct thing from uniformity in
the midst of variety, and is a superior kind of beauty.

It is true, that benevolence to being in general will
naturally incline to justice, or proportion in the exercises of it. He who loves being, simply considered,
will naturally, other things being equal, love particular beings in a proportion compounded of the degree
of being, and the degree of virtue, or benevolence to
being, which they have. And that is to love beings in
proportion to their dignity. For the dignity of any
being consists in those two things. Respect to being,
in this proportion, is the first and most general kind
of justice: which will produce all the subordinate
kinds. So that, after benevolence to being in general
exists, the proportion which is observed in objects
may be the cause of the proportion of benevolence
to those objects; but no proportion is the cause or
ground of the existence of such a thing as benevolence to being. The tendency of objects to excite that
degree of benevolence which is proportionable to the
degree of being, etc. is the consequence of the existence of benevolence, and not the ground of it. Even
as a tendency of bodies, one to another, by mutual
attraction, in proportion to the quantity of matter, is

the consequence of the being of such a thing as mutual attraction; and not attraction the effect of proportion.

By this it appears, that just affections and acts have a beauty in them, distinct from and superior to the uniformity and equality there is in them: for which he that has a truly virtuous temper, relishes and delights in them. And that is the expression and manifestation there is in them of benevolence to being in general. And besides this, there is the agreement of justice to the will and command of God; and also something in the tendency and consequences of justice, agreeable to general benevolence, as the glory of God, and the general good. Which tendency also makes it beautiful to a truly virtuous mind. So that the tendency of general benevolence to produce justice, also the tendency of justice to produce effects agreeable to general benevolence, both render justice pleasing to a virtuous mind. And it is on these accounts chiefly, that justice is grateful to a virtuous taste, or a truly benevolent heart. But though it be true, that the uniformity and proportion there is in justice is grateful to a benevolent heart, as this uniformity and proportion tends to the general good; yet that is no argument that there is no other beauty in it but its agreeing with benevolence. For so the external regularity and order of the natural world gratifies benevolence, as it is profitable, and tends to the general good; but that is no argument that there is no

other sort of beauty in external uniformity and proportion, but only its suiting benevolence, by tending
to the general good.

5. From all that has been observed concerning this
secondary kind of beauty it appears, that the disposition which consists in a determination of mind to approve and be pleased with this beauty, considered
simply and by itself, has nothing of the nature of true
virtue, and is entirely a different thing from a truly
virtuous taste. For it has been shown, that this kind
of beauty is entirely diverse from the beauty of true
virtue, whether it takes place in material or immaterial things; and therefore it will follow, that a taste
of this kind of beauty is entirely a different thing
from a taste of true virtue. Who will affirm, that a
disposition to approve of the harmony of good music,
or the beauty of a square or equilateral triangle, is
the same with true holiness, or a truly virtuous disposition of mind? It is a relish of uniformity and proportion that determines the mind to approve these
things. And there is no need of any thing higher, or
of any thing in any respect diverse, to determine the
mind to approve and be pleased with equal uniformity and proportion among spiritual things which are
equally discerned. It is virtuous to love true virtue,
as that denotes an agreement of the heart with virtue.
But it argues no virtue for the heart to be pleased
with that which is entirely distinct from it.

Though it be true, that there is some analogy in it
to spiritual and virtuous beauty—as far as material

things can have analogy to things spiritual, of which they can have no more than a shadow—yet, as has been observed, men do not approve it because of any such analogy perceived. And not only reason but experience plainly shows, that men's approbation of this sort of beauty does not spring from any virtuous temper, and has no connection with virtue. For otherwise their delight in the beauty of squares, and cubes, and regular polygons, in the regularity of buildings, and the beautiful figures in a piece of embroidery, would increase in proportion to men's virtue; and would be raised to a great height in some eminently virtuous or holy men; but would be almost wholly lost in some others that are very vicious and lewd. It is evident in fact, that a relish of these things does not depend on general benevolence, or any benevolence at all to any being whatsoever, any more than a man's loving the taste of honey, or his being pleased with the smell of a rose. A taste of this inferior beauty in things immaterial, is one thing which has been taken by some moralists, for a true virtuous principle, supposed to be implanted naturally in the hearts of all mankind.

CHAPTER IV

Of Self-Love, and Its Various Influence, to Cause Love to Others, or the Contrary

MANY assert that all love arises from self-love. In order to determine this point, it should be clearly determined what is meant by self-love. Self-love, I think, is generally defined "a man's love of his own happiness"; which is short, and may be thought very plain: but in reality is an ambiguous definition, as the expression his own, is equivocal, and liable to be taken in two very different senses. For a man's own happiness may either be taken universally, for all the happiness or pleasure of which the mind is in any regard the subject, or whatever is grateful and pleasing to men: or it may be taken for the pleasure a man takes in his own proper, private, and separate good. And so self-love may be taken two ways:

1. It may be taken for the same as his loving whatsoever is pleasing to him. Which comes only to this, that self-love is a man's liking, and being suited and pleased in that which he likes, and which pleases him; or, that it is a man's loving what he loves. For whatever a man loves, that thing is grateful and pleasing to him, whether that be his own peculiar happiness, or the happiness of others. And if this be all that they

mean by self-love, no wonder they suppose that all
love may be resolved into self-love. For it is undoubtedly true, that whatever a man loves, his love may be
resolved into his loving what he loves. If by self-love
is meant nothing else but a man's loving what is grateful or pleasing to him, and being averse to what is
disagreeable, this is calling that self-love, which is
only a general capacity of loving or hating; or a capacity of being either pleased or displeased; which is the
same thing as a man's having a faculty of will. For if
nothing could be either pleasing or displeasing, agreeable or disagreeable to a man, then he could incline
to nothing, and will nothing. But if he is capable of
having inclination, will and choice, then what he inclines to and chooses, is grateful to him, whatever
that be; whether it be his own private good, the good
of his neighbours, or the glory of God. And so far as
it is grateful or pleasing to him, so far it is a part of
his pleasure, good, or happiness.

But if this be what is meant by self-love, there is an
impropriety and absurdity even in the putting of the
question, Whether all our love, or our love to each
particular object of our love, does not arise from self-
love? For that would be the same as to enquire,
Whether the reason why our love is fixed on such and
such particular objects, is not, that we have a capacity
of loving some things? This may be a general reason
why men love or hate any thing at all; and therein
differ from stones and trees, which love nothing and
hate nothing. But it can never be a reason why men's

love is placed on such and such objects. That a man in general loves and is pleased with happiness, or has a capacity of enjoying happiness, cannot be the reason why such and such things become his happiness: as for instance, why the good of his neighbour, or the happiness and glory of God, is grateful and pleasing to him, and so becomes a part of his happiness.

Or if what they mean who say that all love comes from self-love, be not that our loving such and such particular persons and things arises from our love to happiness in general, but from a love to our own happiness, which consists in these objects; so, the reason why we love benevolence to our friends or neighbours is because we love our happiness, consisting in their happiness, which we take pleasure in: still the notion is absurd. For here the effect is made the cause of that of which it is the effect: our happiness, consisting in the happiness of the person beloved, is made the cause of our love to that person. Whereas the truth plainly is, that our love to the person is the cause of our delighting, or being happy in his happiness. How comes our happiness to consist in the happiness of such as we love, but by our hearts being first united to them in affection, so that we as it were look on them as ourselves, and so on their happiness as our own? Men who have benevolence to others have pleasure when they see others' happiness, because seeing their happiness gratifies some inclination that was in their hearts before. They before inclined to their happiness; which was by benevolence or good-will; and therefore, when they see their happiness, their inclination is suited, and they are pleased. But the being of inclinations and appetites is prior to any pleasure in gratifying these appetites.

2. Self-love, as the phrase is used in common speech, most commonly signifies a man's regard to his confined private self, or love to himself with respect to his private interest.

By private interest I mean that which most immediately consists in those pleasures, or pains, that are personal. For there is a comfort, and a grief, that some have in others' pleasures or pains; which are in others originally, but are derived to them, or in some measure become theirs, by virtue of a benevolent union of heart with others. And there are other pleasures and pains that are originally our own, and not what we have by such a participation with others. Which consist in perceptions agreeable or contrary to certain personal inclinations implanted in our nature; such as the sensitive appetites and aversions. Such also is the disposition or the determination of the mind to be pleased with external beauty, and with all inferior, secondary beauty, consisting in uniformity, proportion, etc. whether in things external or internal, and to dislike the contrary deformity. Such also is the natural disposition in men to be pleased in a perception of their being the objects of the honour and love of others, and displeased with others' hatred and contempt. For pleasures and uneasiness of this kind are doubtless as much owing to an immediate determina-

tion of the mind by a fixed law of our nature, as any
of the pleasures or pains of external sense. And these
pleasures are properly of the private and personal
kind; being not by any participation of the happiness
or sorrow of others, through benevolence. It is evidently mere self-love that appears in this disposition.
It is easy to see that a man's love to himself will make
him love love to himself, and hate hatred to himself.
And as God has constituted our nature, self-love is
exercised in no one disposition more than in this. Men
probably are capable of much more pleasure and pain
through this determination of the mind, than by any
other personal inclination or aversion whatsoever.
Though perhaps we do not so very often see instances
of extreme suffering by this means as by some others,
yet we often see evidences of men's dreading the contempt of others more than death; and by such instances may conceive something what men would
suffer if universally hated and despised; and may rea-
sonably infer something of the greatness of the misery
that would arise under a sense of universal abhorrence, in a great view of intelligent being in general,
or in a clear view of the Deity, as incomprehensibly
and immensely great, so that all other beings are as
nothing and vanity—together with a sense of his immediate continual presence, and an infinite concern
with him and dependence upon him—and living con-
stantly in the midst of most clear and strong evidences
and manifestations of his hatred and contempt. These
things may be sufficient to explain what I mean by

private interest; in regard to which self-love, most properly so called, is immediately exercised.

And here I would observe, that if we take self-love in this sense, so love to some others may truly be the effect of self-love; i.e. according to the common method and order which is maintained in the laws of nature. For no created thing has power to produce an effect any otherwise than by virtue of the laws of nature. Thus that a man should love those who are of his party, and who are warmly engaged on his side, and promote his interest, is the natural consequence of a private self-love. Indeed there is no metaphysical necessity in the nature of things, that because a man loves himself and regards his own interest, he therefore should love those that love him and promote his interest, i.e. to suppose it to be otherwise implies no contradiction. It will not follow from any absolute metaphysical necessity, that because bodies have solidity, cohesion, and gravitation towards the centre of the earth, therefore a weight suspended on the beam of a balance should have greater power to counterbalance a weight on the other side, when at a distance from the fulcrum, than when it is near. It implies no contradiction that it should be otherwise; but only as it contradicts that beautiful proportion and harmony, which the Author of Nature observes in the laws of nature he has established. Neither is there any absolute necessity, that because there is an internal mutual attraction of the parts of the earth, or any other sphere, whereby the whole becomes one

solid coherent body, therefore other bodies that are
around it should also be attracted by it, and those
that are nearest be attracted most. But according to
the order and proportion generally observed in the
laws of nature, one of these effects is connected with
the other, so that it is justly looked upon as the same
power of attraction in the globe of the earth, which
draws bodies about the earth towards its centre, with
that which attracts the parts of the earth themselves
one to another; only exerted under different circumstances. By a like order of nature, a man's love to those
who love him, is no more than a certain expression or
effect of self-love. No other principle is needful in
order to the effect, if nothing intervenes to countervail
the natural tendency of self-love. Therefore there is
no more true virtue in a man thus loving his friends
merely from self-love, than there is in self-love itself,
the principle from whence it proceeds. So a man being disposed to hate those that hate him, or to resent
injuries done him, arises from self-love, in like manner as loving those that love us, and being thankful
for kindness shown us.

But it is said by some, that it is apparent there is
some other principle concerned in exciting the passions of gratitude and anger besides self-love, viz. a
moral sense, or sense of moral beauty and deformity,
determining the minds of all mankind to approve of,
and be pleased with virtue, and to disapprove of vice,
and behold it with displicence; and that their seeing
or supposing this moral beauty or deformity in the

kindness of a benefactor, or opposition of an adversary, is the occasion of these affections of gratitude or anger. Otherwise, why are not these affections excited in us towards inanimate things that do us good or hurt? Why do not we experience gratitude to a garden, or fruitful field? And why are we not angry with a tempest, or blasting mildew, or an overflowing stream? We are very differently affected towards those that do us good from the virtue of generosity, or hurt us from the vice of envy and malice, than towards things that hurt or help us, which are destitute of reason and will. Concerning this I would make several remarks.

1. Those who thus argue, that gratitude and anger cannot proceed from self-love, might argue in the same way, and with equal reason, that neither can these affections arise from love to others: which is contrary to their own scheme. They say that the reason why we are affected with gratitude and anger towards men, rather than things without life, is moral sense: which they say is the effect of that principle of benevolence or love to others, or love to the public, which is naturally in the hearts of all mankind. But now, I might say, according to their own way of arguing, gratitude and anger cannot arise from love to others, or love to the public, or any sense of mind that is the fruit of public affection. For how differently are we affected towards those who do good or hurt to the public from understanding and will, and public motive, from what we are towards such inanimate

things as the sun and the clouds, that do good to the
public by enlightening and enlivening beams and
refreshing showers; or mildew, and an overflowing
stream, that does hurt to the public by destroying
the fruits of the earth? Yea, if such a kind of argument
be good, it will prove that gratitude and anger cannot arise from the united influence of self-love and
public love, or moral sense arising from public affection. For if so, why are we not affected towards inanimate things that are beneficial or injurious both to us
and the public, in the same manner as to them that
are profitable or hurtful to both on choice and design,
and from benevolence or malice?

2. On the supposition, that men love those who
love them, and are angry with those who hate them,
from the natural influence of self-love; it is not at
all strange that the Author of Nature, who observes
order, uniformity, and harmony in establishing its
laws, should so order, that it should be natural for
self-love to cause the mind to be affected differently
towards exceedingly different objects; and that it
should cause our heart to extend itself in one manner
towards inanimate things, which gratify self-love
without sense or will, and in another manner towards
beings which we look upon as having understanding
and will, like ourselves, and exerting these faculties
in our favour, and promoting our interest from love to
us. No wonder, seeing we love ourselves, that it
should be natural to us to extend something of that
same kind of love which we have for ourselves, to

them who are the same kind of beings as ourselves, and comply with the inclinations of our self-love, by expressing the same sort of love towards us.

3. If we should allow that to be universal, that in gratitude and anger there is the exercise of some kind of moral sense—as it is granted there is something that may be so called—all the moral sense that is essential to those affections, is a sense of *Desert;* which is to be referred to that sense of justice before spoken of, consisting in an apprehension of that secondary kind of beauty that lies in uniformity and proportion; which solves all the difficulty in the objection. Others' love and kindness to us, or their ill-will and injuriousness, appear to us to deserve our love or our resentment. Or in other words, it seems to us no other than just, that as they love us and do us good, we also should love them and do them good. And so it seems just, that when others' hearts oppose us, and they from their hearts do us hurt, our hearts should oppose them, and that we should desire themselves may suffer in like manner as we have suffered, i.e. there appears to us to be a natural agreement, proportion, and adjustment between these things; which is indeed a kind of moral sense, or sense of beauty in moral things. But, as was before shown, it is a moral sense of a secondary kind, and is entirely different from a sense or relish of the original essential beauty of true virtue; and may be without any principle of true virtue in the heart. Therefore, doubtless, it is a great mistake in any to suppose, that the moral sense which

appears and is exercised in a sense of desert, is the same thing as a love of virtue, or a disposition and determination of mind to be pleased with true virtuous beauty, consisting in public benevolence. Which may be further confirmed if it be considered, that even with respect to a sense of justice or desert, consisting in uniformity, and agreement between others' actions towards us and our actions towards them, in a way of well-doing or of ill-doing, it is not absolutely necessary to the being of these passions of gratitude and anger, that there should be any notion of justice in them, in any public or general view of things: as will appear by what shall be next observed.

4. Those authors who hold that the moral sense which is natural to all mankind, consists in a natural relish of the beauty of virtue, and so arises from a principle of true virtue implanted by nature in the hearts of all, hold that true virtue consists in public benevolence. Therefore, if the affections of gratitude and anger necessarily imply such a moral sense as they suppose, then these affections imply some delight in the public good, and an aversion of the mind to public evil. And if so, then every time a man feels anger for opposition, or gratitude for any favour, there must be at least a supposition of a tendency to public injury in that opposition, and a tendency to public benefit in the favour that excites his gratitude. But how far is this from being true? For instance: a ship's crew enter into a conspiracy against the master, to murder him, and run away with the ship, and turn

pirates: but before they bring their matters to ripeness for execution, one of them repents, and opens the whole design; whereupon the rest are apprehended and brought to justice. The crew are enraged with him who has betrayed them, and earnestly seek opportunity to revenge themselves upon him. And for an instance of gratitude; a gang of robbers that have long infested the neighbouring country, have a particular house whither they resort, and where they meet from time to time to divide their booty, and hold their consultations for carrying on their pernicious designs. The magistrates and officers of the country, after many fruitless endeavours to discover their secret place of resort, at length are well-informed where it is, and are prepared with sufficient force to surprise them, and seize them all at the place of rendezvous, at an hour appointed when they understand they will all be there. A little before the arrival of the appointed hour, while the officers with their bands are approaching, some person is so kind to these robbers, as to give them notice of their danger, so as just to give them opportunity to escape. They are thankful to him, and give him a handful of money for his kindness. Now in such instances I think it is plain, that there is no supposition of a public injury in that which is the occasion of their anger; yea, they know the contrary. Nor is there any supposition of public good in that which excites their gratitude; neither has public benevolence, or more sense, consisting in a determination to approve of what is for the public good, any influence at all in the affair. And though there be some affection, besides a sense of uniformity and proportion, that has influence in such anger and gratitude, it is not public affection or benevolence, but private affection; yea, that affection which is to the highest degree private, consisting in a man's love of his own person.

5. The passion of anger, in particular, seems to have been unluckily chosen as a medium to prove a sense and determination to delight in virtue, consisting in benevolence natural to all mankind. For if that moral sense which is exercised in anger, were that which arose from a benevolent temper of heart, being no other than a sense or relish of the beauty of benevolence, one would think a disposition to anger should increase at least in some proportion, as a man had more of a sweet, benign, and benevolent temper: which seems contrary to experience, which shows that the less men have of benevolence, and the more they have of a contrary temper, the more are they disposed to anger and deep resentment of injuries.

And though gratitude be that which many speak of as a certain noble principle of virtue, which God has implanted in the hearts of all mankind; and though it be true there is a gratitude that is truly virtuous: and the want of gratitude, or an ungrateful temper, is truly vicious, and argues an abominable depravity of heart; yet I think, what has been observed may serve to convince such as impartially consider it, not only that not all anger, or hating those which hate us, but also that not all gratitude, or loving those which love us, arises from a truly virtuous benevolence of heart.

Another sort of affections which may be properly referred to self-love as its source, and which might be expected to be the fruit of it, according to the general analogy of nature's laws, is that of affections to such as are near to us by the ties of nature. Such are those of whose beings we have been the occasion, in which we have a very peculiar propriety, and whose circumstances, even from the beginning of their existence, many ways lead them to a high esteem of us, and to treat us with great dependence, submission and compliance. These the constitution of the world makes to be united in interest, and accordingly to act as one, in innumerable affairs, with a communion in each other's affections, desires, cares, friendships, enmities, and pursuits. As to the opinion of those who ascribe the natural affection there is between parents and children to a particular instinct of nature, I shall take notice of it afterwards.

And as men may love persons and things from self-love, so may their love to qualities and characters arise from the same source. Some represent this, as though there were need of a great degree of metaphysical refining to make it out, that men approve of others from self-love, whom they hear of at a distance, or read of in history, or see represented on the stage, from whom they expect no profit or advantage. But perhaps it is not considered, that what we approve of in the first place is the character; and from the character we approve the person. And is it a strange thing, that men should from self-love like a temper or character, which in its nature and tendency falls in with the nature and tendency of self-love; and which we know by experience and self-evidence, without metaphysical refining, in the general tends to men's pleasure and benefit? And on the contrary, it is strange that any should dislike what they see tends to men's pain and misery? Is there need of a great degree of subtlety and abstraction to make it out, that a child, who has heard and seen much of what is calculated strongly to fix an idea of the pernicious, deadly nature of the rattlesnake, should have an aversion to that species from self-love; so as to have a degree of this aversion and disgust excited by seeing even the picture of that animal? And that from the same self-love it should be pleased with a lively representation of some pleasant fruit of which it has often tasted the sweetness? Or with the image of some bird, which it has always been told is innocent, and with whose pleasant singing it has often been entertained? Yet the child neither fears being bitten by the picture of the snake, nor expects to eat of the painted fruit, or to hear the figure of the bird sing. I suppose none will think it difficult to allow, that such an approbation or disgust of a child may be accounted for from its natural delight in the pleasure, of taste and hearing, and its aversion to pain and death, through self-love, together with the habitual connection of these agreeable or terrible ideas with the form and qualities of these objects, the ideas of which are impressed on the mind of the child by their images.

And where is the difficulty of allowing, that a person may hate the general character of a spiteful and malicious man, for the like reason as he hates the general nature of a serpent; knowing from reason, instruction and experience, that malice in men is pernicious to mankind, as well as spite or poison in a serpent? And if a man may from self-love disapprove the vices of malice, envy, and others of that sort, which naturally tend to the hurt of mankind, why may he not from the same principle approve the contrary virtues of meekness, peaceableness, benevolence, charity, generosity, justice, and the social virtues in general; which he as easily and clearly knows, naturally tend to the good of mankind? It is undoubtedly true, that some have a love to these virtues from a higher principle. But yet I think it as certainly true, that there is generally in mankind a sort of approbation of them, which arises from self-love.

Besides what has been already said, the same thing further appears from this; that men commonly are most affected towards, and most highly approve, those virtues which agree with their interest most, according to their various conditions in life. We see that persons of low condition are especially enamoured with a condescending, accessible, affable temper in the great; not only in those whose condescension has been exercised towards themselves; but they will be

peculiarly taken with such a character when they
have accounts of it from others, or when they meet
with it in history, or even in romance. The poor will
most highly approve and commend liberality. The
weaker sex, who especially need assistance and pro-
tection, will peculiarly esteem and applaud fortitude
and generosity in those of the other sex, of whom they
read or hear, or which they have represented to them
on a stage.

I think it plain from what has been observed, that
as men may approve and be disposed to commend a
benevolent temper from self-love; so the higher the
degree of benevolence is, the more may they approve
of it. This will account for some kind of approbation,
from this principle, even of love to enemies, viz. as a
man loving his enemies is an evidence of a high degree of benevolence of temper; the degree of it ap-
pearing from the obstacles it overcomes. And it may
be here observed, that the consideration of the tendency and influence of self-love may show, how men in
general may approve of justice from another ground,
besides that approbation of the secondary beauty
there is in uniformity and proportion, which is natural
to all. Men, from their infancy, see the necessity of it,
not only that it is necessary for others or for human
society; but they find the necessity of it for themselves, in instances that continually occur; which
tends to prejudice them in its favour, and to fix an
habitual approbation of it from self-love.

Again, that forementioned approbation of justice

and desert, arising from a sense of the beauty of natural agreement and proportion, will have a kind of reflex, and indirect influence to cause men to approve benevolence, and disapprove malice; as men see that he who hates and injures others deserves to be hated and punished, and that he who is benevolent, and loves others and does them good, deserves himself also to be loved and rewarded by others, as they see the natural congruity or agreement, and mutual adaptness of these things. And having always seen this, malevolence becomes habitually connected in the mind with the idea of being hated and punished, which is disagreeable to self-love; and the idea of benevolence is habitually connected and associated with the idea of being loved and rewarded by others, which is grateful to self-love. And by virtue of this association of ideas, benevolence itself becomes grateful, and the contrary displeasing.

Some vices may become in a degree odious by the influence of self-love, through an habitual connection of ideas of contempt with it; contempt being what self-love abhors. So it may often bè with drunkenness, gluttony, sottishness, cowardice, sloth, niggardliness. The idea of contempt becomes associated with the idea of such vices, both because we are used to observe that these things are commonly objects of contempt, and also find that they excite contempt in ourselves. Some of them appear marks of littleness, i.e. of small abilities, and weakness of mind, and insufficiency for any considerable effects among mankind.

By others, men's influence is contracted into a narrow sphere, and by such means persons become of less importance, and more insignificant. And things of little importance are naturally little accounted of. And some of these ill qualities are such as mankind find it their interest to treat with contempt, as they are very hurtful to human society. There are no particular moral virtues whatsoever, but what in some or other of these ways, and most of them in several, come to have some kind of approbation from self-love, without the influence of a truly virtuous principle; nor any particular vices, but what, by the same means, meet with some disapprobation.

This kind of approbation and dislike, through the joint influence of self-love and association of ideas, is in many vastly heightened by education. This is the means of a strong, close, and almost irrefragable association, in innumerable instances of ideas, which have no connection any other way than by education; and is the means of greatly strengthening that association or connection which persons are led into by other means: as any one would be convinced, perhaps more effectually than in most other ways, if they had opportunity of any considerable acquaintance with American savages and their children.

CHAPTER V

Of Natural Conscience, and the Moral Sense

THERE is yet another disposition or principle, of great importance, natural to mankind; which, if we consider the consistence and harmony of nature's laws, may also be looked upon as in some sort arising from self-love, or self-union; and that is, a disposition in man to be uneasy in a consciousness of being inconsistent with himself, and as it were against himself in his own actions. This appears particularly in the inclination of the mind to be uneasy in the consciousness of doing that to others, which he should be angry with them for doing to him, if they were in his case, and he in theirs; or of forbearing to do that to them, which he would be displeased with them for neglecting to do to him.

I have observed from time to time, that in pure love to others, i.e. love not arising from self-love, there is an union of the heart with others; a kind of enlargement of the mind, whereby it so extends itself as to take others into a man's self: and therefore it implies a disposition to feel, to desire, and to act as though others were one with ourselves. So, self-love implies an inclination to feel and act as one with ourselves; which naturally renders a sensible inconsistence with

61

ourselves, and self-opposition in what we ourselves choose and do, to be uneasy to the mind: which will cause uneasiness of mind to be the consequence of a malevolent and unjust behaviour towards others, and a kind of disapprobation of acts of this nature, and an approbation of the contrary. To do that to another, which we should be angry with him for doing to us, and to hate a person for doing that to us, which we should incline to and insist on doing to him, if we were exactly in the same case, is to disagree with ourselves, and contradict ourselves. It would be for ourselves both to choose and adhere to, and yet to refuse and utterly reject the very same thing. No wonder this is contrary to nature. No wonder that such a self-opposition, and inward war with a man's self, naturally begets unquietness, and raises disturbance in his mind.

Thus approving of actions, because we therein act as in agreement with ourselves; and thus disapproving, and being uneasy in the consciousness of disagreeing with ourselves in what we do, is quite a different thing from approving or disapproving actions because in them we are united with being in general: which is loving or hating actions from a sense of the primary beauty of true virtue, and of the odiousness of sin. The former of these principles is private; the latter is public, and truly benevolent in the highest sense. The former—an inclination to agree with ourselves—is a natural principle: but the latter—an agreement or union of heart to the great system, and to

God the head of it, who is all and all in it—is a divine principle.

In that uneasiness now mentioned, consists very much of that inward trouble men have from reflections of conscience: and when they are free from this uneasiness, and are conscious to themselves, that in what they have acted towards others, they have done the same which they should have expected from them in the same case, then they have what is called peace of conscience, with respect to these actions. And there is also an approbation of conscience, respecting the conduct of others towards ourselves. As when we are blamed, condemned, or punished by them, and are conscious to ourselves that if we were in their case and they in ours, we should in like manner, blame, condemn, and punish them. And thus men's consciences may justify God's anger and condemnation. When they have the ideas of God's greatness, their relation to him, the benefits they have received from him, the manifestations he has made of his will to them, etc. strongly impressed on their minds, a consciousness is excited within them of those resentments, which would be occasioned in themselves by an injurious treatment in any wise parallel.

There certainly is such a consciousness as this oftentimes within men, implied in the thoughts and views of the mind, of which perhaps on reflection, they could hardly give an account. Unless men's consciences are greatly stupified, it is naturally and necessarily suggested; and habitually, spontaneously, instantaneously, and as it were insensibly arises in the mind. And the more so for this reason, that we have no other way to conceive of any thing which other persons act or suffer, but by recalling and exciting the ideas of what we ourselves are conscious we have found in our own minds; and by putting the ideas which we obtain by this means in the place of another; or as it were, substituting ourselves in their place. Thus we have no conception, what understanding, perception, love, pleasure, pain, or desire are in others; but by putting ourselves as it were in their stead, or transferring the ideas we obtain of such things in our own minds by consciousness into their place; making such an alteration, as to degree and circumstances, as what we observe of them requires. It is thus in all moral things that we conceive of in others; and indeed in every thing we conceive of belonging to others, more than shape, size, complexion, situation, and motion of their bodies. And this is the only way that we come to be capable of having ideas of any perception or act even of the Godhead. We never could have any notion what understanding or volition, love or hatred are, either in created spirits or in God, if we had never experienced what understanding and volition, love and hatred are in our own minds. Knowing what they are by consciousness, we can deny limits, and remove changeableness and other imperfections, and ascribe them to God.

But though men in thinking of others do as it were put themselves in their place, they do it so habitually, instantaneously, and without set purpose, that they can scarce give any account of it, and many would think it strange if they were told of it. In all a man's thoughts of another person, in whatever he apprehends of his moral conduct to others or to himself, if it be in loving or hating him, approving or condemning him, rewarding or punishing him, he necessarily as it were, puts himself in his stead; and therefore the more naturally, easily, and quietly sees whether he, being in his place, should approve or condemn, be angry or pleased as he is.

Natural conscience consists in these two things.

1. In that disposition to approve or disapprove the moral treatment which passes between us and others, from a determination of the mind to be easy or uneasy, in a consciousness of our being consistent or inconsistent with ourselves. Hereby we have a disposition to approve our own treatment of another, when we are conscious to ourselves that we treat him so as we should expect to be treated by him, were he in our case and we in his; and to disapprove of our own treatment of another, when we are conscious that we should be displeased with the like treatment from him, if we were in his case. So we in our consciences approve of another's treatment of us, if we are conscious to ourselves, that if we were in his case, and he in ours, we should think it just to treat him as he treats us; and disapprove his treatment of us, when we are conscious that we should think it unjust, if we were in his case. Thus men's consciences approve

or disapprove the sentence of their judge, by which
they are acquitted or condemned. But this is not all
that is in natural conscience. Besides this approving
or disapproving from uneasiness as being inconsistent
with ourselves, there is another thing that must pre-
cede it, and be the foundation of it. As for instance,
when my conscience disapproves my own treatment
of another, being conscious to myself, that were I in
his case, I should be displeased and angry with him
for so treating me; the question might be asked, What
would be the ground of that supposed disapprobation,
displeasure, and anger, which I am conscious would
be in me in that case? Therefore,

2. The other thing which belongs to the approbation or disapprobation of natural conscience, is the
sense of desert which was spoken of before; consisting
as was observed, in a natural agreement, proportion
and harmony, between malevolence or injury, and
resentment and punishment; or between loving and
being loved, between shewing kindness and being
rewarded, etc. Both these kinds of approving or disapproving concur in the approbation or disapprobation of conscience: the one founded on the other.
Thus when a man's conscience disapproves of his
treatment of his neighbour, in the first place he is conscious, that if he were in his neighbour's stead, he
should resent such treatment from a sense of justice,
or from a sense of uniformity and equality between
such treatment, and resentment, and punishment; as
before explained. And then in the next place, he per-

ceives that therefore he is not consistent with himself, in doing what he himself should resent in that
case; and hence disapproves it, as being naturally
averse to opposition to himself.

Approbation and disapprobation of conscience, in
the sense now explained, will extend to all virtue and
vice; to every thing whatsoever that is morally good
or evil, in a mind which does not confine its view to
a private sphere, but will take things in general into
its consideration, and is free from speculative error.
For as all virtue or moral good may be resolved into
love to others, either God or creatures, so men easily
see the uniformity and natural agreement there is between loving others, and being accepted and favoured
by others. And all vice, sin, or moral evil summarily
consisting in the want of this love to others, or in
malevolence; so men easily see the natural agreement
there is between hating and doing ill to others, and
being hated by them, and suffering ill from them, or
from him that acts for all, and has the care of the
whole system. And as this sense of equality and natural agreement extends to all moral good and evil;
so this lays a foundation of an equal extent with the
other kind of approbation and disapprobation, which
is grounded upon it, arising from an aversion to self-
inconsistence and opposition. For in all cases of benevolence or the contrary towards others, we are
capable of putting ourselves in the place of others,
and are naturally led to do it; and so of being conscious to ourselves, how we should like or dislike such

treatment from others. Thus natural conscience, if
the understanding be properly enlightened, and stupi-
fying prejudices are removed, concurs with the law
of God, is of equal extent with it, and joins its voice
with it in every article.

And thus, in particular, we may see in what respect
this natural conscience extends to true virtue, consisting in union of heart to being in general, and supreme
love to God. For although it sees not, or rather does
not taste its primary and essential beauty, i.e. it tastes
no sweetness in benevolence to being in general, simply considered, for nothing but general benevolence
itself can do that, yet this natural conscience, common to mankind, may approve of it from that uniformity, equality and justice, which there is in it; and
the demerit which is seen in the contrary, consisting
in the natural agreement between the contrary, and
being hated of being in general. Men, by natural conscience, may see the justice or natural agreement,
there is in yielding all to God, as we receive all from
him; and the justice there is in being his that made
us, and willingly so, which is the same as being dependent on his will, and conformed to it in the manner of our being; as we are for our being itself, and
in the conformity of our will to his, on whose will we
are universally and most perfectly dependent. There
is also justice in our supreme love to God; a natural
agreement in our having a supreme respect to him
who exercises infinite goodness to us, and from whom

NATURAL CONSCIENCE AND THE MORAL SENSE 69

we receive all well-being. Besides disagreement and
discord appears worse to natural sense in things nearly related, and of great importance: and therefore it
must appear very ill, as it respects the infinite Being,
and in that infinitely great relation which there is between the Creator and his creatures. And it is easy to
conceive how natural conscience should see the desert
of punishment, in the contrary of true virtue, viz.
opposition and enmity to being in general. For this is
only to see the natural agreement there is between
opposing being in general, and being opposed by being in general; with a consciousness how, if we were
infinitely great, we should expect to be regarded according to our greatness, and should proportionably
resent contempt. This natural conscience, if well-
informed, will approve of true virtue, and will disapprove and condemn the want of it, and opposition to
it; and yet without seeing the true beauty of it. Yea, if
men's consciences were fully enlightened, if they were
delivered from being confined to a private sphere,
and brought to view and consider things in general,
and delivered from being stupified by sensual objects
and appetites, as they will be at the day of judgment,
they would approve nothing but true virtue, nothing
but general benevolence and those affections and actions that are consistent with it, and subordinate to it.
For they must see that consent to being in general,
and supreme respect to the Being of beings, is most
just; and that every thing which is inconsistent with

it, and interferes with it, or flows from the want of it, is unjust and deserves the opposition of universal existence.

Thus has God established and ordered that this principle of natural conscience, which, though it implies no such thing as actual benevolence to being in general, nor any delight in such a principle, simply considered, and so implies no truly spiritual sense or virtuous taste, yet should approve and condemn the same things that are approved and condemned by a spiritual sense or virtuous taste. And that moral sense which is natural to mankind, so far as it is disinterested, and not founded in association of ideas, is the same with this natural conscience.

The sense of moral good and evil, and that disposition to approve virtue and disapprove vice, which men have by natural conscience, is that moral sense so much insisted on in the writings of many of late. A misunderstanding of this seems to have misled those moralists, who have insisted on a disinterested moral sense, universal in the world of mankind, as an evidence of a disposition to true virtue, consisting in a benevolent temper, naturally implanted in the minds of all men. Some of the arguments used by these writers, indeed prove that there is a moral sense or taste, universal among men, distinct from what arises from self-love. Though I humbly conceive there is some confusion in their discourses on the subject, and not a proper distinction observed in the instances of men's approbation of virtue which they produce. Some of which are not to their purpose, being instances of that approbation of virtue which arises from self-love. But other instances prove, that there is a moral taste, or sense of moral good and evil, natural to all, which do not properly arise from self-love. Yet I conceive there are no instances of this kind which may not be referred to natural conscience, and particularly to that which I have observed to be primary in the approbation of natural conscience, viz. a sense of desert, and approbation of that natural agreement there is, in manner and measure in justice. But I think it is plain from what has been said, that neither this, nor any thing else wherein consists the sense of moral good and evil which there is in natural conscience, is of the nature of a truly virtuous taste, or determination of mind to relish and delight in the essential beauty of true virtue, arising from a virtuous benevolence of heart.

But it further appears from this; if the approbation of conscience were the same with the approbation of the inclination of the heart, or the natural disposition and determination of the mind to love and be pleased with virtue, then approbation and condemnation of conscience would always be in proportion to the virtuous temper of the mind; or rather, the degree would be just the same. In that person who had a high degree of a virtuous temper, therefore, the testimony of conscience in favour of virtue would be equally full: But he who had but little, would have as little a degree of the testimony of conscience for virtue, and against vice. But I think the case is evidently otherwise. Some men, through the strength of vice in their hearts, will go on in sin against clearer light and stronger convictions of conscience than others. If conscience, approving duty and disapproving sin, were the same thing as the exercise of a virtuous principle of the heart, in loving duty and hating sin, then remorse of conscience will be the same thing as repentance; and just in the same degree as the sinner feels remorse of conscience for sin, in the same degree is the heart turned from the love of sin to the hatred of it, inasmuch as they are the very same thing.

Christians have the greatest reason to believe, from the scriptures, that in the future day of the revelation of the righteous judgment of God, when sinners shall be called to answer before their judge, and all their wickedness, in all its aggravations, brought forth and clearly manifested in the perfect light of that day; and God will reprove them, and set their sins in order before them, their consciences will be greatly awakened and convinced, their mouths will be stopped, all stupidity of conscience will be at an end, and conscience will have its full exercise; and therefore their consciences will approve the dreadful sentence of the judge against them; and seeing that they have deserved so great a punishment, will join with the judge in condemning them. And this according to the notion I am opposing, would be the same thing as their being brought to the fullest repentance; their hearts being perfectly changed to hate sin and love holiness; and

virtue or holiness of heart in them will be brought to
the most full and perfect exercise. But how much
otherwise have we reason to suppose it will then be?
Then the sin and wickedness of their heart will come
to its highest dominion and completest exercise; they
shall be wholly left of God, and given up to their
wickedness, even as the devils are! When God has
done waiting on sinners, and his Spirit done striving
with them, he will not restrain their wickedness, as he
does now. But sin shall then rage in their hearts, as a
fire no longer restrained or kept under. It is proper
for a judge when he condemns a criminal, to endeavour so to set his guilt before him as to convince his
conscience of the justice of the sentence. This the
Almighty will do effectually, and do to perfection, so
as most thoroughly to awaken and convince the conscience. But if natural conscience and the disposition
of the heart to be pleased with virtue, were the same,
then at the same time that the conscience was brought
to its perfect exercise, the heart would be made perfectly holy; or would have the exercise of true virtue
and holiness in perfect benevolence of temper. But
instead of this, their wickedness will then be brought
to perfection, and wicked men will become very devils, and accordingly will be sent away as cursed into
everlasting fire prepared for the devil and his angels.

But supposing natural conscience to be what has
been described, all these difficulties and absurdities
are wholly avoided. Sinners when they see the greatness of the being in contempt of whom they have

lived with rebellion and opposition and have clearly set before them their obligations to him as their Creator, preserver, benefactor, etc. together with the degree in which they have acted as enemies to him, may have a clear sense of the desert of their sin, consisting in the natural agreement there is between such contempt and opposition of such a being, and his despising and opposing them; between their being and acting as so great enemies to such a God, and their suffering the dreadful consequences of his being and acting as their great enemy; and their being conscious within themselves of the degree of anger, which would naturally arise in their own hearts in such a case, if they were in the place and state of their judge. In order to these things, there is no need of a virtuous benevolent temper, relishing and delighting in benevolence, and loathing the contrary. The conscience may see the natural agreement between opposing and being opposed, between hating and being hated, without abhorring malevolence from a benevolent temper of mind, or without loving God from a view of the beauty of his holiness. These things have no necessary dependence one on the other.

CHAPTER VI

Of Particular Instincts of Nature, Which in Some Respects Resemble Virtue

THERE are various dispositions and inclinations natural to men, which depend on particular laws of nature, determining their minds to certain affections and actions towards particular objects; which laws seem to be established chiefly for the preservation of mankind, and their comfortably subsisting in the world. These dispositions may be called instincts.

Some of these instincts respect only ourselves personally: such are many of our natural appetites and aversions. Some of them are more social, and extend to others: such are the mutual inclinations between the sexes, etc. Some of these dispositions are more external and sensitive: such are those that relate to meat and drink, and the more sensitive inclinations of the sexes towards each other. Others are more internal and mental: consisting in affections which mankind naturally exercise towards some of their fellow-creatures, and in some cases towards men in general. Some of these may be called kind affections; as having something in them of benevolence, or a resemblance of it: and others are of an angry appearance; such as the passion of jealousy between the sexes, especially in the male towards the female.

It is only the former of these two last mentioned sorts that it is to my purpose to consider in this place, viz. those natural instincts which have the appearance of benevolence and so in some respects resemble virtue. These I shall therefore consider; and shall endeavour to show, that none of them can be of the nature of true virtue.

That kind affection which is exercised one towards another in natural relation, particularly the love of parents to their children, called natural affection, is by many referred to instinct. I have already considered this sort of love as an affection that arises from self-love: and in that view, have shown it cannot be of the nature of true virtue. But if any think, that natural affection is more properly to be referred to a particular instinct of nature than to self-love, as its cause, I shall not think it a point worthy of any controversy or dispute. In my opinion both are true; viz. that natural affection is owing to natural instinct, and also that it arises from self-love. It may be said to arise from instinct, as it depends on a law of nature. But yet it may be truly reckoned as an affection arising from self-love; because, though it arises from a law of nature, yet that is such a law as according to the order and harmony every where observed among the laws of nature, is connected with, and follows from self-love; as was shown before. However, it is not necessary to my present purpose to insist on this. For if natural affection to a man's children or near

relations, is an affection arising from a particular independent instinct of nature—which the Creator in
his wisdom has implanted in men for the preservation and well-being of the world of mankind: yet it
cannot be of the nature of true virtue. For it has been
observed, and I humbly conceive, proved before
(Chap. II), that if any being or beings have by natural instinct, or any other means, a determination of
mind to benevolence, extending only to some particular persons or private system, however large that system may be—or however great a number of individuals it may contain, so long as it contains but an
infinitely small part of universal existence, and so
bears no proportion to this great and universal system
—such limited private benevolence, not arising from,
not being subordinate to benevolence to being in general, cannot have the nature of true virtue. However,
it may not be amiss briefly to observe now, that it is
evident to a demonstration those affections cannot be
of the nature of true virtue, from these two things.

First, That they do not arise from a principle of
virtue. A principle of virtue, I think, is owned by the
most considerable of late writers on morality to be
general benevolence or public affection: and I think
it has been proved to be union of heart to being simply considered; which implies a disposition to benevolence to being in general. Now by the supposition,
the affections we are speaking of do not arise from
this principle; and that, whether we suppose they
arise from self-love, or from particular instinct: be-

cause either of those sources is diverse from a principle of general benevolence. And,

Secondly, These private affections, if they do not
arise from general benevolence, and they are not connected with it in their first existence, have no tendency to produce it. This appears from what has been
observed: for being not dependent on it, their detached and unsubordinate operation rather implies
opposition to being in general, than general benevolence; as every one sees and owns with respect to
self-love. And there are the very same reasons why
any other private affection, confined to limits infinitely
short of universal existence, should have that influence, as well as love that is confined to a single person. Now upon the whole, nothing can be plainer
than that affections which do not arise from a virtuous
principle, and have no tendency to true virtue as their
effect, cannot be of the nature of true virtue.

For the reasons which have been given, it is undeniably true, that if persons have a benevolent affection limited to a party, or to the nation in general of
which they are a part, or the public community to
which they belong, though it be as large as the Roman
empire was of old: yea, if there could be a cause
determining a person to benevolence towards the
whole world of mankind, or even all created sensible
natures throughout the universe, exclusive of union
of heart to general existence and of love to God—not
derived from that temper of mind which disposes to
a supreme regard to him, nor subordinate to such

divine love—it cannot be of the nature of true virtue.

If what is called natural affection arises from a particular natural instinct, much more indisputably does that mutual affection which naturally arises between the sexes. I agree with Hutchison and Hume in this, that there is a foundation laid in nature for kind affections between the sexes, diverse from all inclinations to sensitive pleasure, and which do not properly arise from any such inclination. There is doubtless a disposition both to a mutual benevolence and mutual complacence, that are not naturally and necessarily connected with any sensitive desires. But yet it is manifest such affections as are limited to opposite sexes, are from a particular instinct thus directing and limiting them; and not arising from a principle of general benevolence; for this has no tendency to any such limitation. And though these affections do not properly arise from the sensitive desires which are between the sexes, yet they are implanted by the Author of Nature chiefly for the same purpose, viz. the preservation or continuation of the world of mankind. Hereby persons become willing to forsake father and mother, and all their natural relations in the families where they were born and brought up, for the sake of a stated union with a companion of the other sex, in bearing and going through that series of labours, anxieties, and pains, requisite to the being, support, and education of a family of children; and partly also for the comfort of mankind as united in a marriage-relation. But I suppose, few, if any, will deny, that the peculiar natural dispositions there are to mutual affection between the sexes, arise from an instinct or particular law of nature. And therefore it is manifest, from what has been said already, that those natural dispositions cannot be of the nature of true virtue.

Another affection, which is owing to a particular instinct, is that pity which is natural to mankind when they see others in great distress. It is acknowledged, that such an affection is natural to mankind. But I think it evident, that the pity which is general and natural, is owing to a particular instinct, and is not of the nature of true virtue. I am far from saying that there is no such thing as a truly virtuous pity among mankind; or that none is to be found, which arises from that truly virtuous divine principle of general benevolence to sensitive beings. Yet at the same time I think, this is not the case with *all* pity, or with that disposition to pity which is natural to mankind in common. I think I may be bold to say, this does not arise from benevolence, nor is it properly called by that name.

If all that uneasiness on the sight of others' extreme distress which we call pity, were properly of the nature of benevolence, then they who are the subjects of this passion, must needs be in a degree of uneasiness, in being sensible of the total want of happiness of all such as they would be disposed to pity in extreme distress. For that certainly is the most direct tendency and operation of benevolence or good will, to desire the happiness of its object. But now this is not the case universally, where men are disposed to exercise pity. There are many who would not be sensibly affected with any uneasiness to know that others were dead, yea, men who are not influenced by the consideration of a future state, but view death as only a cessation of all sensibility, and consequently an end of all happiness—who yet would have been moved with pity towards the same persons, if they had seen them under some very extreme anguish. Some would be moved with pity by seeing a brute-creature under extreme and long torments, who yet suffer no uneasiness in knowing that many thousands of them every day cease to live, and so have an end put to all their pleasure. It is the nature of true benevolence to desire and rejoice in the prosperity and pleasure of its object; and that in some proportion to its degree of prevalence. But persons may greatly pity those that are in extreme pain, whose positive pleasure they may still be very indifferent about. In this case, a man may be much moved and affected with uneasiness, who yet would be affected with no sensible joy in seeing signs of the same person's enjoyment of very high degrees of pleasure.

Yea, pity may not only be without benevolence, but may consist with true malevolence, or with such ill will as shall cause men not only to desire the positive happiness of another, but even to desire his calamity. They may pity such an one when his calamity goes beyond their hatred. A man may have true malevolence towards another, desiring no positive good for him, but evil; and yet his hatred not be infinite, but only to a certain degree. And when he sees the person whom he thus hates in misery far beyond his ill will, he may then pity him: because then the natural instinct begins to operate. For malevolence will not overcome the natural instinct inclining to pity others in extreme calamity, any further than it goes, or to the limits of the degree of misery it wishes to its object. Men may pity others under exquisite torment, when yet they would have been grieved if they had seen their prosperity. And some have such a grudge against another, that they would be far from uneasy at their very death, nay, would even be glad of it. And when this is the case, it is manifest that their heart is void of benevolence towards such persons, and under the power of malevolence. Yet at the same time, they are capable of pitying even these very persons, if they should see them under a degree of misery very much disproportioned to their ill will.

These things may convince us, that natural pity is of a nature very different from true virtue, and not arising from a disposition of heart to general benevolence; but is owing to a particular instinct, which the Creator has implanted, chiefly for the preservation of mankind, though not exclusive of their well being. The giving of this instinct is the fruit of God's mercy, and an instance of his love to the world of mankind, and an evidence, that though the world be so sinful, it is not God's design to make it a world of punishment; and therefore has many ways made a merciful provision of relief in extreme calamities. The natural exercises of pity extend beyond those with whom we are nearly connected, especially in cases of great calamity; because commonly in such cases, men stand in need of the help of others besides their near friends, and because commonly those calamities which are extreme, without relief, tend to their destruction. This may be given as the reason why men are so made by the Author of Nature, that they have no instinct inclining as much to rejoice at the sight of others' great prosperity and pleasure, as to be grieved at their extreme calamity, viz. because they do not stand in equal necessity of such an instinct as that in order to their preservation. But if pure benevolence were the source of natural pity, doubtless it would operate to as great a degree in congratulation, in cases of others, great prosperity, as in compassion towards them in great misery.

The instincts which in some respects resemble a virtuous benevolence, are agreeable to the state that God designed mankind for here, where he intends their preservation and comfortable subsistence. But in the world of punishment—where the state of the wicked inhabitants will be exceeding different, and God will have none of these merciful designs to answer—we have great reason to think, there will be no such thing as a disposition to pity, in any case; as also no natural affection towards near relations, and no mutual affection between opposite sexes.

To conclude, natural instinct, disposing men to pity others in misery, is also a source of a kind of abhorrence in men of some vices, as cruelty and oppression; and so of a sort of approbation of the contrary virtues, humanity, mercy, etc. which aversion and approbation however, so far as they arise from this cause only, and not from a principle of true virtue.

CHAPTER VII

*The Reasons Why Those Things That Have Been
Mentioned, Which Have Not the Essence
of Virtue, Have Yet by Many Been
Mistaken for True Virtue*

THE first reason may be this, that although they have
not the specific and distinguishing nature and essence
of virtue, yet they have something that belongs to the
general nature of virtue. The general nature of true
virtue is love. It is expressed both in love of benevolence and complacence; but primarily in benevolence
to persons and beings, and consequently and second-
arily in complacence in virtue, as has been shown.
There is something of the general nature of virtue in
those natural affections and principles that have been
mentioned, in both those respects.

In many of these natural affections there appears
the tendency and effect of benevolence in part. Others have truly a sort of private benevolence, but which
in several respects falls short of the extent of true virtuous benevolence, both in its nature and object. Pity
to others in distress, though not properly of the nature
of love, as has been demonstrated, yet has partly the
same influence and effect with benevolence. One effect of true benevolence is for persons to be uneasy

when the objects of it are in distress, and to desire their relief. And natural pity has the same effect.

Natural gratitude, though not properly called love —because persons may be moved with a degree of gratitude towards others on certain occasions for whom they have no real and proper friendship; as in the instance of Saul towards David, once and again, after David's sparing his life when he had so fair opportunity to kill him—yet has the like operation and effect with friendship, in part, for a season, and with regard to so much of the welfare of its object, as appears a deserved requital of kindness received. And in other instances, it may have a more general and abiding influence, so as more properly to be called by the name of love. So that many times men, from natural gratitude, do really with a sort of benevolence, love those who love them. From this, together with some other natural principles, men may love their near friends, their own party, their country, etc. The natural disposition there is to mutual affection between the sexes, often operates by what may properly be called love. There is oftentimes truly a kind both of benevolence and complacence. As there also is between parents and children.

Thus these things have something of the general nature of virtue. What they are essentially defective in is, that they are private in their nature; they do not arise from any temper of benevolence to being in general, nor have they a tendency to any such effect in their operation. But yet agreeing with virtue in its general nature, they are beautiful within their own private sphere, i.e. they appear beautiful if we confine our views to that private system, and while we shut out all other things to which they stand related from our consideration. If that private system contained the sum of universal existence, their benevolence would have true beauty; or in other words, would be beautiful, all things considered; but now it is not so. These private systems are so far from containing the sum of universal being, or comprehending all existence to which we stand related, that it contains but an infinitely small part of it. The reason why men are so ready to take these private affections for true virtue, is the narrowness of their views; and above all, that they are so ready to leave the divine Being out of their view, and to neglect him in their consideration, or to regard him in their thoughts as though he did not properly belong to the system of real existence, but was a kind of shadowy, imaginary being. And though most men allow that there is a God, yet in their ordinary view of things, his being is not apt to come into the account, and to have the influence and effect of a real existence, as it is with other beings which they see, and are conversant with by their external senses. In their views of beauty and deformity, and in their inward sensations of displicence and approbation, it is not natural to them to view the Deity as part of the system, and as the head of it, in comparison of whom all other things are to be viewed with corresponding impressions.

Yea, we are apt, through the narrowness of our views, in judging of the beauty of affections and actions, to limit our consideration to only a small part of the created system. When private affections extend themselves to a considerable number, we are ready to look upon them as truly virtuous, and accordingly to applaud them highly. Thus it is with respect to a man's love to a large party, or a country. For though his private system contains but a small part even of the world of mankind, yet being a considerable number, they—through the contracted limits of his mind, and the narrowness of his views—are ready to engross his sight, and to seem as if they were all. Hence, among the Romans, love to their country was the highest virtue; though this affection of theirs so much extolled, was employed as it were for the destruction of the rest of mankind. The larger the number is, to which that private affection extends, the more apt men are, through the narrowness of their sight, to mistake it for true virtue; because then the private system appears to have more of the image of the universal.

And this is the reason why self-love is not mistaken for true virtue. For though there be something of the general nature of virtue in it, as love and good will, yet the object is so private, the limits so narrow, that it by no means engrosses the view; unless it be of the person himself, who through the greatness of his pride may imagine himself as it were all. The minds of men are large enough to take in a vastly greater extent. And though self-love is far from being use-less in the world, yea, it is exceeding necessary to society; yet every body sees that if it be not subordi-nate to, and regulated by another more extensive principle, it may make a man a common enemy to the general system. And this is as true of any other private affection, notwithstanding its extent may be to a system that contains millions of individuals. And though private systems bear no greater proportion to the whole of universal existence, than one alone; yet they bear a greater proportion to the view and com-prehension of men's minds, and are more apt to be regarded as if they were all, or at least as some resem-blance of the universal system.

Thus I have observed how many of these natural principles resemble virtue in its primary operation, which is benevolence. Many of them also have a re-semblance of it in its secondary operation, which is its approbation of, and complacence in virtue itself. Several kinds of approbation of virtue are not of the nature of a truly virtuous approbation, consisting in a sense and relish of the essential beauty of virtue. As particularly, the approbation of conscience, from a sense of the inferior and secondary beauty which there is in virtue, consisting in uniformity; and from a sense of desert, consisting in a sense of the natural agreement of loving and being beloved, shewing kind-ness and receiving kindness. So from the same princi-ple, there is a disapprobation of vice, from a natural opposition to deformity and disproportion; and a sense of evil desert, or the natural agreement there is between hating and being hated, opposing and being opposed, etc. together with a painful sensation naturally arising from a sense of self-opposition and inconsistence. Approbation of conscience is the more readily mistaken for a truly virtuous approbation, because by the wise constitution of the great Governor of the world, when conscience is well informed and thoroughly awakened, it agrees with him fully and exactly as to the object approved, though not as to the ground and reason of approving. It approves all virtue, and condemns all vice. It approves true virtue and indeed approves nothing that is against it, or that falls short of it; as was shown before. Natural conscience is implanted in all mankind, to be as it were in God's stead, as an internal judge or rule, whereby to distinguish right and wrong.

It has also been observed, how that virtue, consisting in benevolence, is approved; and vice, consisting in ill will, is disliked; from the influence of self-love, together with the association of ideas. In the same manner men dislike those qualities in things without life or reason, with which they have always connected the ideas of hurtfulness, malignancy, perniciousness; but approve those things with which they habitually connect the ideas of profit, pleasantness, etc. This approbation of virtue and dislike of vice, is easily mistaken for true virtue, not only because those things are approved by it that have the nature of virtue, and the things disliked have the nature of vice; but be-

cause here is a great resemblance of virtuous approbation, it being complacence from love; the difference
only lying in this, that it is not from love to being in
general, but from self-love.

There is also, as before shown, a liking of some virtues and a dislike of some vices, from the influence of
the natural instinct of pity. This we are apt to mistake
for the exercise of true virtue on many accounts.
Here is not only a kind of complacence, and the objects of complacence have the nature of virtue, and
the virtues themselves are very amiable, such as humanity, mercy, tenderness of heart, etc. and the contrary very odious; but besides, the approbation is not
merely from self-love, but from compassion; an affection that respects others, and resembles benevolence,
as before explained.

Another reason why the things mentioned are mistaken for true virtue, is, that there is indeed a true
negative moral goodness in them. By a negative moral
goodness, I mean the negation or absence of true
moral evil. They have this negative moral goodness,
because being without them would be an evidence
of a much greater moral evil. Thus the exercise of
natural conscience in such and such degrees, wherein
appears such a measure of sensibility, though it be
not of the nature of real positive virtue, or true moral
goodness, yet has a negative moral goodness; because
in the present state of things, it is an evidence of the
absence of that higher degree of wickedness, which
causes great insensibility, or stupidity of conscience.

For sin is not only against a spiritual and divine sense of virtue, but is also against the dictates of that moral sense which is in natural conscience. No wonder that this sense, being long opposed and often conquered, grows weaker. All sin has its source from selfishness, or from self-love not subordinate to a regard to being in general. And natural conscience chiefly consists in a sense of desert, or the natural agreement between sin and misery. But if self were indeed all, and so more considerable than all the world besides, there would be no ill desert in a man regarding himself above all, and making all other interests give place to private interest. And no wonder that men, by long acting from the selfish principle, and by being habituated to treat themselves as if they were all, increase in pride, and come to look on themselves as all, and so to lose entirely the sense of ill desert in their making all other interests give place to their own. And no wonder that any, by often repeating acts of sin without punishment, or visible appearance of approaching punishment, have less and less present sense of the connection of sin with punishment.

That sense which an awakened conscience has of the desert of sin, consists chiefly in a sense of its desert of resentment from the Deity, the fountain and head of universal existence. But no wonder that by a long continued worldly and sensual life, men more and more lose all sense of the Deity, who is a spiritual and invisible Being. The mind being long involved in, and engrossed by sensitive objects, becomes sensual in all its operations, and excludes all views and impressions of spiritual objects, and is unfit for their contemplation. Thus conscience and general benevolence are entirely different principles; and thus a sense of conscience differs from the holy complacence of a benevolent and truly virtuous heart. Yet wickedness may by long habitual exercise greatly diminish a sense of conscience. So that there may be negative moral goodness in sensibility of conscience, as it may be an argument of the absence of that higher degree of wickedness, which causeth stupidity of conscience.

So with respect to natural gratitude; though there may be no virtue merely in loving them that love us, yet the contrary may be an evidence of a great degree of depravity, as it may argue a higher degree of selfishness, so that a man is come to look upon himself as all, and others as nothing, and so their respect and kindness as nothing. Thus an increase of pride diminishes gratitude. So doth sensuality, or the increase of sensual appetites; which coming more and more under the power and impression of sensible objects, tends by degrees to make the mind insensible to any thing else. Those appetites take up the whole soul; and, through habit and custom, the water is all drawn out of other channels in which it naturally flows, and is all carried as it were into one channel.

In like manner, natural affection, and natural pity, though not of the nature of virtue, may be diminished greatly by the increase of pride and sensuality; and as the consequence of this, be habitually disposed to envy, malice, etc. These lusts, when they prevail to a high degree, may overcome and diminish the exercise of those natural principles; even as they often overcome and diminish common prudence in a man, who seeks his own private interest in point of health, wealth, or honour; and yet no one will think it proves that a man being cunning in seeking his own personal and temporal interest, has any thing of the nature and essence of true virtue.

Another reason why these natural principles and affections are mistaken for true virtue, is, that in several respects they have the same effect which true virtue tends to; especially in these two ways:

1. The present state of the world is so constituted by the wisdom and goodness of its supreme Ruler, that these natural principles, for the most part, tend to the good of mankind. So do natural pity, gratitude, parental affection, etc. Herein they agree with the tendency of general benevolence, which seeks and tends to the general good. But this is no proof that these natural principles have the nature of true virtue. For self-love is exceeding useful and necessary; and so are the natural appetites of hunger, thirst, etc. Yet nobody will assert that these have the nature of true virtue.

2. These principles have a like effect with true virtue in this respect, that they tend several ways to restrain vice, and prevent many acts of wickedness. So natural affection, love to our party, or to particular friends, tends to keep us from acts of injustice

towards these persons; which would be real wicked-ness. Pity preserves from cruelty, which would be real and great moral evil. Natural conscience tends to restrain sin in general. But this cannot prove these principles themselves to be of the nature of true vir-tue. For so is this present state ordered by a merciful God, that even self-love often restrains from acts of true wickedness; and not only so, but puts men upon seeking true virtue; yet is not itself true virtue, but is the source of all the wickedness that is in the world.

Another reason why these inferior affections, espe-cially some of them, are accounted virtuous, is, that there are affections of the same denomination which are truly virtuous. Thus, for instance, there is a truly virtuous pity, or a compassion to others under afflic-tion or misery, from general benevolence. Pure benev-olence would be sufficient to excite pity to another in calamity, if there were no particular instinct, or any other principle determining the mind thereto. It is easy to see how benevolence, which seeks another's good, should cause us to desire his deliverance from evil. And this is a source of pity far more extensive than the other. It excites compassion in cases that are overlooked by natural instinct; and even in those cases to which instinct extends, it mixes its influence with the natural principle, and guides and regulates its operations. And when this is the case, the pity which is exercised may be called a virtuous compas-sion. So there is a virtuous gratitude; or a gratitude that arises not only from self-love, but from a superior

principle of disinterested general benevolence. As
when we receive kindness from such as we love already, we are more disposed to gratitude, and disposed to greater degrees of it, than when the mind is
destitute of any such friendly prepossession. Therefore when the superior principle of virtuous love has
a governing hand, and regulates the affair, it may be
called a virtuous gratitude. There is also a virtuous
love of justice, arising from pure benevolence to being
in general; as that naturally and necessarily inclines
the heart, that every particular being should have
such a share of benevolence as is proportioned to its
dignity, consisting in the degree of its being and the
degree of its virtue. And thus it is easy to see, how
there may be a virtuous sense of desert different from
what is natural and common; and a virtuous con-
scientiousness, or a sanctified conscience. And as,
when natural affections have their operations mixed
with the influence of virtuous benevolence, and are
directed and determined thereby, they may be called
virtuous; so there may be a virtuous love of parents
to children, and between other near relatives; a virtuous love of our town, or country, or nation. Yea, and
a virtuous love between the sexes, as there may be
the influence of virtue mingled with instinct; and virtue may govern with regard to the particular manner
of its operation, and may guide it to such ends as are
agreeable to the great purposes of true virtue.

Genuine virtue prevents that increase of the habits
of pride and sensuality, which tend to diminish the

exercises of the useful and necessary principles of nature. And a principle of general benevolence softens and sweetens the mind, makes it more susceptible of the proper influence of the gentler natural instincts, directs every one into its proper channel, determines the exercise to the proper manner and measure, and guides all to the best purposes.

CHAPTER VIII

*In What Respects Virtue or Moral Good Is
Founded in Sentiment; and How Far
It Is Founded in the Reason and
Nature of Things*

VIRTUE is a certain kind of beautiful nature, form, or quality. That form or quality is called beautiful, which appears in itself agreeable or comely, or the view of which is immediately pleasant to the mind. I say agreeable in itself, and immediately pleasant, to distinguish it from things which in themselves are not so, but either indifferent or disagreeable; which yet appear eligible and agreeable indirectly, for something else with which they are connected. Such indirect agreeableness or eligibleness in things not for themselves, but for something else, is not beauty. But when a form or quality appears lovely, pleasing and delightful in itself, then it is called beautiful; and this agreeableness or gratefulness of the idea is *beauty*. It is evident that the way we come by the idea of beauty is by immediate sensation of the gratefulness of the idea called beautiful; and not by finding out by argumentation any consequences, or other things with which it stands connected; any more than tasting the sweetness of honey, or perceiving the harmony of a tune, is by argumentation on connections and consequences. The manner of being affected with the immediate presence of the beautiful idea, depends not on any reasonings about the idea after we have it, before we can find out whether it be beautiful or not; but on the frame of our minds, whereby they are so made that such an idea, as soon as we have it, is grateful, or appears beautiful.

Therefore, if this be all that is meant by them who affirm that virtue is founded in sentiment, and not in reason, that they who see the beauty of true virtue do not perceive it by argumentation on its connections and consequences, but by the frame of their own minds, or a certain spiritual sense given them of God —whereby they immediately perceive pleasure in the presence of the idea of true virtue in their minds, or are directly gratified in the view or contemplation of this object—this is certainly true. But if thereby be meant, that the frame of mind, or inward sense given them by God, whereby the mind is disposed to delight in the idea of true virtue, is given arbitrarily, so that if he had pleased he might have given a contrary sense and determination of mind, which would have agreed as well with the necessary nature of things, this I think is not true.

Virtue, as I have observed, consists in the cordial consent or union of being to being in general. And that frame of mind, whereby it is disposed to relish and be pleased with the view of this, is benevolence or union of heart to being in general; or it is an uni-

versally benevolent frame of mind. Because he whose
temper is to love being in general, must therein have
a disposition to approve and be pleased with love
to being in general. Therefore now the question is,
Whether God, in giving this temper to a created mind,
acts so arbitrarily, that there is nothing in the necessary nature of things to hinder, but that a contrary
temper might have agreed or consisted as well with
that nature of things as this?

And in the first place, to assert this would be a plain
absurdity, and contrary to the very supposition. For
here it is supposed, that virtue in its very essence
consists in agreement or consent of being to being.
Now certainly agreement itself to being in general
must necessarily agree better with general existence,
than opposition and contrariety to it.

I observe, secondly, that God in giving to the creature such a temper of mind, gives that which is agreeable to what is by absolute necessity his own temper
and nature. For, as observed, God himself is in effect
being in general; and without all doubt it is in itself
necessary, that God should agree with himself, be
united with himself, or love himself: and therefore,
when he gives the same temper to his creatures, this
is more agreeable to his necessary nature, than the
opposite temper: yea, the latter would be infinitely
contrary to his nature.

Let it be noted, thirdly, that by this temper only
can created beings be united to, and agree with one
another. This appears because it consists in consent

and union to being in general; which implies agreement and union with every particular being, except in such cases wherein union with them is by some means inconsistent with union to general existence. But certainly, if any particular created being were of a temper to oppose being in general, that would infer the most universal and greatest possible discord, not only of creatures with their Creator, but of created beings one with another.

Fourthly, There is no other temper but this, whereby a man can agree with himself, or be without self-inconsistence, i.e. without having some inclinations and relishes repugnant to others; and that for these reasons. Every being that has understanding and will, necessarily loves happiness. For to suppose any being not to love happiness, would be to suppose he did not love what was agreeable to him; which is a contradiction: or at least would imply, that nothing was agreeable or eligible to him, which is the same as to say that he has no such thing as choice, or any faculty of will. So that every being who has a faculty of will, must of necessity have an inclination to happiness. And therefore, if he be consistent with himself, and has not some inclinations repugnant to others, he must approve of those inclinations whereby beings desire the happiness of being in general, and must be against a disposition to the misery of being in general: because otherwise he would approve of opposition to his own happiness. For if a temper inclined to the misery of being in general prevailed universally, it is apparent, it would tend to universal misery. But he that loves a tendency to universal misery, in effect loves a tendency to his own misery: and as he necessarily hates his own misery, he has then one inclination repugnant to another. And besides, it necessarily follows from self-love, that men love to be loved by others; because in this others' love agrees with their own love. But if men loved hatred to being in general, they would in effect love the hatred of themselves; and so would be inconsistent with themselves, having one natural inclination contrary to another.

These things may help us to understand why that spiritual and divine sense, by which those who are truly virtuous and holy perceive the excellency of true virtue, is in the sacred scriptures called by the name of light, knowledge, understanding, etc. If this divine sense were a thing arbitrarily given, without any foundation in the nature of things, it would not properly be called by such names. For if there were no correspondence or agreement in such a sense with the nature of things, any more than there would have been in a contrary sense, the idea we obtain by this spiritual sense could in no respect be said to be a knowledge or perception of any thing besides what was in our own minds. For this idea would be no representation of any thing without. But since it is agreeable, in the respects abovementioned, to the nature of things; and especially since it is the representation of the moral perfection and excellency of the divine Being; hereby we have a perception of that moral ex-

cellency, of which we could have no true idea without
it. And hereby persons have that true knowledge of
God, which greatly enlightens the mind in the knowledge of divine things in general, and which, as might
be shown if it were necessary to the main purpose of
this discourse, in many respects assists persons to a
right understanding of things in general; viz. to see
the nature and truth of them, in their proper evidence.
Whereas, the want of this spiritual sense, and the
prevalence of those dispositions which are contrary to
it, tends to darken and distract the mind, and dread-
fully to delude and confound men's understandings.

Nor can that moral sense common to mankind,
which there is in natural conscience, be truly said to
be no more than a sentiment, arbitrarily given by the
Creator, without any relation to the necessary nature
of things: but rather this is established in agreement
with the nature of things; so established, as no sense
of mind that can be supposed of a contrary nature
and tendency could be. This will appear by these two
things:

1. This moral sense—if the understanding be well
informed, exercised at liberty, and in an extensive
manner, without being restrained to a private sphere
—approves the very same things which a spiritual and
divine sense approves; and those things only; though
not on the same grounds, nor with the same kind of
approbation. Therefore, as that divine sense is agreeable to the necessary nature of things, as already
shown; so this inferior moral sense, being so far cor-

respondent to that, must also so far agree with the nature of things.

2. It has been shown, that this moral sense consists in approving the uniformity and natural agreement there is between one thing and another. So that, by the supposition, it is agreeable to the nature of things. For therein it consists, viz. a disposition of mind to consent to or like, the agreement of the nature of things, or the agreement of the nature and form of one thing with another. And certainly, such a temper of mind is more agreeable to the nature of things than an opposite temper.

The use of language is to express our *sentiments,* or ideas, to each other; so that those terms by which things of a moral nature are signified, express those moral sentiments which are common to mankind. Therefore, that *moral sense* which in its natural conscience, chiefly governs the use of language, and is the mind's rule of language in these matters. It is indeed the general natural rule which God has given to all men, whereby to judge of moral good and evil. By such words, right and wrong, good and evil, when used in a moral sense, is meant in common speech, that which deserves praise or blame, respect or resentment; and mankind in general have a sense of desert, by this natural moral sense.

Therefore here is a question which may deserve to be considered: Seeing sentiment is the rule of language, as to what is called good and evil, worthy and unworthy; and it is apparent that sentiment, at least as to many particulars, is different in different persons, especially in different nations—that being thought to deserve praise by one, which by others is thought to be worthy of blame—how therefore can virtue and vice be any other than arbitrary; not at all determined by the nature of things, but by the sentiments of men with relation to the nature of things?

In order to the answering of this question with clearness, it may be divided into two: viz. Whether men's sentiments of moral good and evil are casual and accidental? And, whether their way of using words in what they call good and evil, is not arbitrary, without respect to any common sentiment conformed to the nature of things?

As to the first I would observe that the general disposition or sense of mind, exercised in a sense of desert of esteem or resentment, may be the same in all: though as to particular objects and occasions with regard to which it is exercised, it may be very various in different men or bodies of men, through the partiality or error that may attend the view or attention of the mind. In all a notion of desert of love or resentment, may consist in the same thing in general—a suitableness, or natural uniformity and agreement between the affections and acts of the agent, and the affection and treatment of others some way concerned —and yet occasions and objects through a variety of apprehensions about them, and the various manner in which they are viewed, by reason of the partial attention of the mind, may be extremely various. Besides, example, custom, education, and association, may contribute to this, in ways innumerable. But it is needless to enlarge here, since what has been said by others, Mr. Hutchison in particular, may abundantly show, that the differences which are to be found among different persons and nations concerning moral good and evil, are not inconsistent with a general moral sense, common to all mankind.

Nor, secondly, is the use of the words, good and evil, right and wrong, when used in a moral sense, altogether unfixed and arbitrary, according to the variety of notions, opinions and views, that occasion the forementioned variety of sentiment. For though the signification of words is determined by particular use, yet that which governs in the use of terms, is general or common use. And mankind, in what they would signify by terms, are obliged to aim at a consistent use; because it is easily found that the end of language, which is to be a common medium of manifesting ideas and sentiments, cannot be obtained any other way than by a consistent use of words; both that men should be consistent with themselves, and one with another, in the use of them. But men cannot call any thing right or wrong, worthy or ill-deserving, consistently, any other way than by calling things so, which truly deserve praise or blame, i.e. things wherein, all things considered, there is most uniformity in connecting with them praise or blame. There is no other way in which they can use these terms consistently with themselves. Thus if thieves or traitors may be angry with informers that bring them to justice, and call their behaviour by odious names; yet herein they are inconsistent with themselves; because when they put themselves in the place of those who have injured them, they approve the same things they condemn. And therefore, such are capable of being convinced, that they apply these odious terms in an abusive manner. So a nation that prosecutes an ambitious design of universal empire, by subduing other nations with fire and sword, may affix terms that signify the highest degrees of virtue, to the conduct of such as show the most engaged, stable, resolute spirit in this affair, and do most of this bloody work. But yet they are capable of being convinced that they use these terms inconsistently, and abuse language in it, and so having their mouths stopped. And not only will men use such words inconsistently with themselves but also with one another, by using them any otherwise than to signify true merit or ill deserving, as before explained. For there is no way else wherein men have any notion of good or ill desert, in which mankind in general can agree. Mankind in general seem to suppose some general standard, or foundation in nature, for an universal consistence in the use of the terms whereby they express moral good and evil; which none can depart from but through error and mistake. This is evidently supposed in all their disputes about right and wrong; and in all endeavours used to prove that any thing is either good or evil, in a moral sense.

SELECTED ANN ARBOR PAPERBACKS
works of enduring merit

For a complete list of Ann Arbor Paperback titles write:
THE UNIVERSITY OF MICHIGAN PRESS / ANN ARBOR